NATURALS

To the
Robert Redford
of Fly Fishing
Merry Christmas
Love
Diane & Paul
& Meredith
1987

NATURALS

A Guide to Food Organisms of the Trout

Gary A. Borger

DRAWINGS BY ROBERT H. PILS

Stackpole Books

NATURALS: FOOD ORGANISMS OF THE TROUT
Copyright © 1980 by
Gary A. Borger

Published by
STACKPOLE BOOKS
Cameron and Kelker Streets
P.O. Box 1831
Harrisburg, Pa. 17105

Published simultaneously in Don Mills, Ontario, Canada
by Thomas Nelson & Sons, Ltd.

Library of Congress Cataloging in Publication Data

Borger, Gary A   1944-
  Naturals, food organisms of the trout.

  Bibliography: p.
  Includes index.
  1. Trout fishing.   2. Insects, Aquatic.   3. Trout—
Food.   4. Flies, Artificial.   I. Title.
SH687.B66   1980   799.1′7′55   79-23099
ISBN 0-8117-1006-8

Printed in the U.S.A.

To Nancy and Jason,
my fishing family,
who supported this project
with enthusiasm and love

Contents

Foreword

The subject of what, when, where, and how trout feed has interested trout fishers throughout the world for several hundred years. The sport of fly fishing and fly-tying is particularly concerned with imitating trout foods, so a knowledge of trout food is extremely practical for the trout fisher. To accomodate this trout fishing sport there has been a multitude of books, stories, and articles, generated by various writers, artists, promoters, and exploiters of the sport.

Yet, unfortunately, the facts show that most of these works have served to communicate little more than a large mass of confusing, useless facts and biased opinions to the average trout fly fisher. (This is not just my opinion but based on the opinions of tens of thousands of trout fly fishermen I speak with each year.) Nearly all of the writings I had read until Swisher and Richard's *Selective Trout* actually muddied my understanding of the trout's world and cooled my enthusiasm about the sport. Their book became a clear, true, objective milestone for matching and fishing natural trout foods.

The impact and perspective of *Selective Trout* raised most major works published afterward to a much higher plane. Still the confusion syndrome of this pleasingly complicated sport persisted. Anglers I communicated with still floundered in the attempt to develop a working familiarity with trout feeding and foods. Even the simple and truly useful facts about stream life can become a confusing mass to the newcomer to the sport, when mixed with technical terms. Indeed, most texts are written more to impress the expert than teach the beginner.

When I first met Gary Borger he was giving an aquatic entomology lecture to a large group of Trout Unlimited members. His lecture cut the fog and confusion of the subject with surprising and refreshing clearness. I learned something new in almost every statement he made that day!

Gary speaks and writes on trout fly fishing subjects with a remarkably easy-to-understand, interesting, and authoritative style to which anyone can relate. His blend of technical biological knowledge and unusually fine fly fishing and tying abilities create a one-in-a-million ability to teach us.

For several years now I have listened to and consulted with Gary. He has been invaluable to my work and personal pleasures of trout fishing. A good example of Gary's special ability on trout food subjects is his adult Poly-Caddis. This one caddis design has out-produced any other six proven caddis adult designs I've used in recent years. It is a design that is almost impossible to fish wrongly. His knowledge of the natural caddis adult and his mastery of the art of tying and fishing are evident in this single fly.

This book is the best of Borger. It is like spending a year at his side. It contains a priceless spectrum you can use concerning what, where, when, and how trout feed. With Borger's way you will be very close to reaching your personal goal in trout fishing.

DAVE WHITLOCK

Acknowledgments

For His help, my most grateful thanks.

The drawings in this book are by my close friend Bob Pils, who has shared with me many hours of his streamside companionship. He deserves special thanks for contributing his considerable artistic talents to this book.

Howard West, a dear friend and marketing supervisor for Scientific Anglers/3M, originally suggested this book and has advanced and supported it with his ideas and friendship. Thanks Howard!

Dick Gaumer, public relations and advertising manager for Fenwick/Woodstream, has been an avid backer of this book. His continual, unrestricted encouragement and warm friendship are deeply appreciated.

Dave Whitlock, internationally known fly fisher, saw this manuscript when it was in the first stages of development. His enthusiastic support has carried through to this final version. For your special friendship, contributions, and efforts on my behalf, thanks Dave.

Nick Lyons deserves grateful acknowledgments for helping me find a publisher.

Special thanks, also, to Alison Brown, associate editor; Jerry Hoffnagle, sales manager; and Neil McAleer, editorial director, at Stackpole Books for their talented assistance in making this book a reality.

My wife, Nancy, willingly typed the first draft of this book even though she openly admits to a fervent dislike of typing. Such unselfishness cannot go unacknowledged.

Bonnie Pils deserves thanks for helping to type the final manuscript.

To friends who have brought me samples and shared insights, thank you.

Some of the material in this book is excerpted from articles written by the author and first appearing in the following publications: Fenwick's *Lunker Gazette, Fly Fisherman, Fly Fishing the West, Proceedings Upper Midwest Trout Symposium I* and *II, Scientific Anglers Fly Fishing Handbook* (first and second editions), *Rod and Reel,* and *Roundtable.* I wish to acknowledge their permission to use this material.

1

From Organism to Imitation

Fly fishers have always been students of nature. Juliana Berners, the Eve of fly fishing, described natural insects and their imitations. Charles Cotton, the disciple of Walton and father of modern fly fishing, also linked his imitations to their natural counterparts. And so it must be since fly fishing is predicated on imitating the trout's food organisms.

The amazing diversity of aquatic life in the streams and lakes of this country seems to be both a blessing and a curse for the fly fisher: a blessing because a large amount of food is available for trout, a curse because the angler has to sort out just which food organisms occur in the waters he fishes and which are most important as trout fodder. Because this task seems so difficult, many anglers tend to go back to the same spot where fish were taken on a previous trip, use one fly again and again because it was successful in the past, and repetitiously ply tactics that have yielded trout.

Actually, collecting, preserving, and identifying food organisms of the trout are fascinating adjuncts to fly fishing. Every fly fisher must be able to identify the major groups of food organisms, and the drawings and descriptions in this book will greatly help with these basics. The common and scientific names of the organisms will also serve as a key to unlock the information stored in angling texts, which very often hold the answer to a seemingly unresolvable angling problem. The serious angler will want to go further and learn as much as possible about the mosaic of life into which the fish is intricately woven. Fishing an artificial fly with *consistent* success requires knowledge of the structure of the organism, its habits, the rhythms of its life cycle, how it appears to the trout, and which of its features induce the fish to feed.

When it comes to eating, the trout, like all animals, is an opportunist. Al McClane points this out almost poetically in *The Practical Fly Fisherman:* "If you examine a trout's stomach it will be evident that whatever the air [or water] is full of, the trout is full of. Fish are like vacuum cleaners working on a stone floor and a liquid ceiling." The types of organisms eaten by the trout, then, depend in large part simply upon their availability. If there are a hundred mayfly nymphs to every stonefly nymph, more mayflies will be eaten. Availability also varies with the life cycle and habits of an organism. Many insects have a one-year life cycle, and in the fall and winter are too small to be important as trout food. Insects having a two- to four-year life cycle are available to the trout all year. Burrowing organisms and those that colonize the undersides of stones are not as vulnerable as drifting invertebrates. Size may be a determining factor since larger prey is more easily seen than smaller prey. Motion is one of the primary triggers of the predatory instincts of the trout; a swimming or drifting organism will be seen and taken sooner than a stationary one. Then, too, trout seem to delight in doing the unpredictable. If both large insects and small ones are available, the fish may choose the smaller. It may be true there are more smaller ones, but why don't the fish eat both types? The big ones would certainly be a bigger mouthful.

Trout will ingest worms, fish eggs, insects, leeches, crustaceans, snails, other fish, frogs, and even small mammals and snakes. Insects, crustaceans, and small fish are most often consumed since they are most often available. Insects important in the trout's diet include those that spend all or part of their lives in the aquatic system and those terrestrial insects that stray into the trout's domain. Overall, the most important aquatic insects are mayflies, stoneflies, caddisflies, and midges. However, depending upon their occurrence in a specific region, craneflies, dragonflies, damselflies, dobsonflies, alderflies, fishflies, and aquatic species of true bugs, beetles, and moths can also be of great significance. Trout prey on all available stages of the life cycles of aquatic insects, even the egg masses. Thus, understanding the peculiarities of a specific insect — its habitat, immature forms, emergence characteristics, adult traits, and size and color at each stage — is of great importance to the serious fly fisherman. Trout also feed readily on such terrestrial insects as ants, beetles, jassids, grasshoppers, and inchworms. Their significance to the angler depends, quite simply, on whether they occur in the water being fished.

To catch trout on flies, it is enough to know that the insect is a mayfly, caddisfly, stonefly, or whatever; its size, color, and shape; and the time it appears on the stream. However, a further understanding of its life cycle and habits will bring the *consistent* success and total comprehension sought by the serious angler.

The size, shape, color, and activity of each stage in the insect's life are the four building blocks out of which imitations are fashioned and tactics developed. Size from one stage to the next can vary greatly, and unless the angler is aware of this difference, the artificials may be too large or small. For most insects, there is a ten to fifty percent reduction in size from the immature to the adult form. However, adult dragonflies, damselflies, true bugs, grasshoppers, and crickets are significantly larger than their immature forms. Shape is often critical in the trout's selection of food, and it's the shape of the natural in or on the water that's important, not the shape the organism assumes when the angler picks it up. Trout see color and can be very choosy about it. The natural motion of an organism is the trait that is perhaps the least understood and least utilized by anglers. Tactics are always aimed at the perfection of the dead drift or drag-free float, but actually the majority of food organisms consumed by trout move. Most anglers fail with the moving fly, however, because they move it too far too fast. Twitches of an inch punctuated with rests of a few seconds take far more fish than a rapidly stripped fly. Of course there are exceptions; that's why it's important to know how the natural moves.

Understanding the life cycle of an organism includes knowing not only the shapes and sizes of the stages but also their durations. Eggs may not hatch for months after being deposited (diapause), or they may hatch rapidly. Nymphs may grow to a large size in only a few months or grow slowly over one or more years. Most aquatic species metamorphose into adults during a well-defined period, which has direct bearing on angling and on the collection of specimens. If you sample a water system over the course of a year, you will find that the species composition varies markedly from month to month. The organisms with a two-year or longer life cycle will be present in all samples, and fishing imitations of these organisms will be successful any time of the year. Eggs and young nymphs or larvae of species having a one-year life cycle may undergo diapause and complete their growth very rapidly in the month or so prior to the time of emergence to the adult. If samples are taken during the diapause of a certain species, that species can very likely be overlooked. Samples taken just prior to the major hatching period of a given species will show large numbers of the species, while samples taken immediately after the hatch will not contain any specimens of the species. Such samplings can lead to false conclusions if the life cycles of the various aquatic organisms are not understood.

From an understanding of an organism's anatomy, habits, and life cycle comes an understanding of the stages to be imitated and the structures to be stressed in the patterns. For example, from his studies, Vince Marinaro was convinced that the wing of the mayfly dun was the key to success, a theory that Swisher and Richards emphasized in their patterns.

In selecting and developing imitations, anglers should keep several criteria in mind: that the artificial give the best impression of the natural, that the fly's design be as simple as possible, that the artificial be rugged, and that the materials be generally available from supply houses. To satisfy the first criterion, the peculiarities of each organism must be noted: silhouette, movement, ovipositing method, colors of naturals in and on the water, behavior of free drifting nymphs or larvae, and feeding patterns of the fish. From such observations, reasons for the success of many conventional patterns will become evident; occasionally these reasons are different from the original logic behind the pattern's development. When developing new patterns, observations are succeeded by experimentation, varying the materials and tying procedures. Completed patterns should be compared with the natural in the aquatic environment. Those artificials that give the best impression of the natural are then tested by actual fishing. The patterns given in the appendix have all been rigorously scrutinized this way.

The developer of a pattern should be more an impressionist than a stark realist. This idea of impressionism in trout flies should be credited to John Atherton, American artist and noted angler. In *The Fly and the Fish,* Atherton states:

> The flies used for so discriminating a fish as the trout should, first of all, have the appearance of life. I am convinced that a lifelike effect can never be obtained by using materials which lack that quality. Impressionism in the materials as well as in the form of flies offers great advantages because it is based on the principles and discoveries of the impressionist painters. As they studied the form which reflected or absorbed light and thus took on certain color qualities of its surroundings, they were dealing in life, not death. Anglers should do the same.

The skeleton of an insect is on the outside of its body and is composed of translucent proteins and chitin, much like fingernails. Not only do the pigments deposited in the exoskeleton color the insect, but microscopic, parallel ridges on the surface diffract the light, giving iridescence to the color. Thin plates on the surface produce the same effect by interference, as does an oil film on water. In addition, any color in the internal organs (such as egg sacks) will glow through the translucent exoskeleton adding another dimension. With modern technology, dyes and molds could replicate insects in plastic, rubber, or metal, but these shams lack a living appearance and are consistently poor baits. Impressions in fur and feather are more effective than exacting models because the natural materials mimic the translucent, iridescent glow of life that was so ardently sought by the impressionists.

To create this impression, it is important to know which features of a food organism trigger selectivity in trout. The trout's eye has evolved to distinguish contrast and motion, not minute detail; size and color discrimination are also well developed. Thus, the trout keys in on size, color, silhouette, and motion (or lack of it). Sometimes one of these traits figures far more prominently in inducing selectivity to a particular organism than do the others. During caddis emergence, for example, the motion of the pupa is most important. Many times the silhouette of terrestrial insects is most significant. Color can be the determining factor for minnow imitations, and size can make a real difference for small insects. Many times not one trait but two, three, or all four are examined by the trout before it takes the organism. The most consistently successful patterns are those that mimic all four characteristics.

The ability to perceive color plays an important role in the feeding habits of fish. Conditioned to accept red food, fish will strike a red lure and shun other colors of the same lure. Furthermore, the fish will retain the color preference for several days even though they have not been shown the red food. This "color hangover" is in part responsible for the trout's selectivity during periods when one food organism is abnormally abundant, such as during a hatch. Trout can distinguish at least twenty-four different hues in addition to complementary colors, shades of gray, brightness, and color contrast. They also see slightly further into the violet region of the spectrum than does man.

In 1972, Bob Pils and I put together a color chart for standardizing our color descriptions of aquatic insects. It was made from printers' color guides as is the one recently marketed by Caucci and Nastasi. For the past eight years we have been testing it extensively across the United States. Several interesting observations have emerged during this time. We proved to ourselves with finality that trout are color conscious, but we also proved that the color of the fly does not have to be matched with absolute precision. There are a number of reasons for this: insects of one species vary slightly in color from one individual to the next, and there can be variations with age, sex, length of time from the previous molt, and the surface on which the insect is living. In addition, the trout may be viewing the fly in dim light or against the sun. We found, too, that one component of an organism's color can be more important than the others. For example, tan scuds often have a hint of orange in them; fluorescent orange blended about half and half in the dubbing makes a better fly than if just a hint of orange is added. The spinners of the Sulphur mayflies are best tied with fluorescent orange bodies rather than yellowish orange ones. Fluorescent purple is good mixed in with black, and so on. Lastly, color is sometimes not the prime feature being selected. These findings have not led us away from the conviction that color is important, but they have tempered it a bit and convinced us that there is still a lot to be learned in this arena. We dropped many color swatches from the original guide, narrowed many selections, and added to some colors, especially grays, creams, tans, and browns.

In an overall sense, we have found that as long as the fly is within a shade or two of the natural, it will be successful. If we don't have an imitation that is the same color as the organism, we choose the closest color. This scheme has proved itself too many times to be only happenstance.

Night fishing is another story because trout, like man, are color blind after dark. Black flies present a very good silhouette against faint starlight (remember the trout is often looking up), and many night anglers prefer dark flies. Reds, yellows, and peacock green have proved to be good colors also. For dry flies, white is often chosen because the angler can see it.

The last word is not yet in on color sensitivity in trout, for man cannot see through the fish's eyes. From our vantage, however, we can be sure that trout are capable of discerning and discriminating among colors.

We can also be sure that the more we all understand of the trout and his world, the more consistent our angling success will be.

2

The Angler as Entomologist

Successful fly fishing requires that the angler understand the meshing of the life cycles of all the organisms in a water system. Obtaining a list of organisms in the system is the prerequisite to establishing the annual rhythm of life. Collecting must take place all throughout the angling season. Collection and identification are followed by relating the organisms to the time of year they are most significant as trout food. Stream records are extremely valuable in this process.

Collection need not become a tedious chore that has to be accomplished before you can allow yourself to fish. After all, fishing trips are supposed to be fun. If they can also be informative, so much the better. Keep your eyes open and take a little time now and then during the course of the day to sample the invertebrate fauna.

As a fly fisherman catalogs the organisms in the waters he fishes, monitors their life cycles, and changes flies and tactics to fit each situation as it develops, he must be continually open minded and be able to recognize important events. Recognition requires knowledge that can be gained by reading, by talking with other anglers, and by experience. Recognition also requires observation, an investment of time that yields greater fishing competency and pleasure. Take time to keep thorough field notes, perform stomach autopsies, catalog the food organisms on home waters, watch the fish, and see the natural world.

Fig. 2–1. A stomach pump for trout

Events must be recorded as they occurred, not as it is wished or supposed they occurred. For example, to the casual onlooker, a rising trout may seem to be feeding on floating insects. In fact, the fish may be feeding on nymphs just under the surface, and even a flawlessly presented dry fly will not be accepted. When large and small insects are on the water together, the trout may be selecting the smaller ones, but the angler might mistakenly assume the larger ones are being taken. Many such instances occur, and the angler has to be alert to what is actually happening.

All my collection gear fits into one vest pocket: stomach pump, white plastic dish, 10X hand lens, small tweezers, vials of alcohol for killing specimens, dry vials for collecting live specimens, and surface and aerial nets. To me this gear is as valuable as my fly boxes.

Stomach autopsies are an excellent source of information on the types of organisms occurring in a stream and on trends in food preferences. Killing fish is not required for analysis of their stomach contents, for a handy little stomach pump with a suction bulb is available from several supply houses. This device removes the stomach contents without injury to the fish (fig. 2–1).

Certain simple and basic precautions should be taken during a stomach pumping session. Most important is to prevent injury to the delicate gills, for once they are ruptured, the fish is in serious straits. Here is the method I have used on many trout with no observed mortality or serious injury. Net the fish with a cotton or soft nylon landing net. Hard nylon or plastic net bags are an abomination; they remove scales and invite infections. Expose the trout's head, roll him several turns in the net bag, and hold him gently underwater; the fish rarely struggles when held this way. If no net is available, hold the trout gently underwater in your hand. Squeezing the fish will only damage its internal organs and cause it to wiggle violently. Depress the bulb and fill the pump about one-fourth full of water. Insert the tube of the pump into the fish's gullet by carefully twisting and pushing, taking exceptional care not to catch the gill arches. Push it down the gullet to the stomach (about one-third of the way back the fish's body) and carefully squeeze the bulb of the pump to flood the gut. If the pump is filled more than one-quarter full, too much water may be left in the fish's stomach and cause physiological distress. Release the bulb, sucking the contents of the upper stomach into the tube. Withdraw the tube and expulse the contents into a white container for viewing. I use the bottom portion of a plastic margarine or cottage cheese tub, trimming the tub's sides to one-half inch. With very little practice, fish eight inches long and longer can be quickly pumped.

Subaquatic forms can be collected with a sampling screen. Such a device is easily made from a three-foot-long piece of standard screen door screening (nylon screening is best, but metal screening will work). Attach a heavy dowel rod to each end to form handles. Place the sampling screen crossways to the current with one end of the handles on the bottom. The other ends of the handles are held above the surface by the person conducting the sampling procedure. The stream bottom is then actively disturbed immediately upstream of the screen with a hoe, garden rake, shovel, stick, or other device or by scuffing in the bottom with your feet. The dislodged organisms will be carried downstream and trapped on the screen. Then, lift the screen from the water and examine the trapped specimens. A kitchen sieve may be similarly used for sampling small areas of the bottom. Additionally, organisms may be hand-picked from rocks, logs, or other bottom structures that have been pulled from the water.

Organisms floating on the surface are very difficult to pick up with the fingers, so I use a simple surface screen. The four-by-five to four-by-six-inch rectangular holders on which plastic models are cast make fine, lightweight frames for this screen. Remove any nubs from the frame and file smooth. If you cannot obtain such a frame, bend one from a wire coat hanger, whipping the ends with cord to secure them. Use nylon bridal veil or similar nylon gauze for the screening. I normally glue it onto the frame, but my good friend Bob Pelzl has found a better method. He sews a flat, rectangular sock of gauze that is open on one side and just large enough that the frame can be slipped in. After the frame is inserted, the fourth side is sewn shut. This

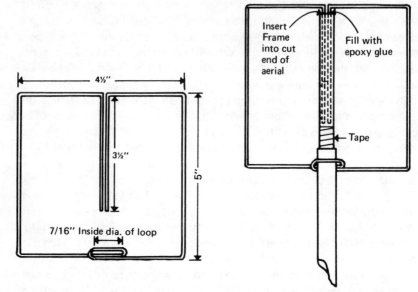

Fig. 2–2. Detail of the wire hoop of the collapsible insect net

Fig. 2–3. Method of attachment of wire hoop to telescoping handle

screen is easily used with one hand. Held in the surface film, it allows the water to pass through while trapping any drifting organisms.

Aerial forms may be captured with a hat or grabbed with your hand, but such radical procedures frequently break off the insects' tails or legs, which may be necessary for identification. A small net with a collapsible handle can be constructed for catching flying insects. The handle is made from a walkie-talkie antenna: the one I use was purchased from Radio Shack. This aerial consists of ten segments and collapses to a length of six and one-half inches. To form the telescoping handle, extend the five *thinnest* segments and place a band of tape around the base of the fifth segment. The tape prevents that segment from falling back inside the sixth segment. Cut through the *fourth* segment at its base and push the stub of this cut end down inside the fifth segment. This handle extends to thirty-one inches, allowing the angler a total reach of about six feet. The hoop of the net is formed from a wire coat hanger to the dimensions indicated in figure 2–2. Coat the ends of the wire with epoxy cement and insert them into the end of the fifth segment of the antenna (fig. 2–3). When the glue has cured, remove the tape from the base of the fifth segment. Make the net bag of nylon bridal veil and sew a border of seam binding along the top. The finished bag should be six to eight inches deep. Fold the seam binding over the wire frame and stitch in place to complete the net (fig. 2–4). Collapsed, this net is as easily stowed as a fly box. Extended and used along the stream, it has often helped me solve the problem of matching the hatch.

Organisms collected from stomach autopsies or with a stomach pump are quite usable if they have not been partially digested.

Not just any specimen is suitable for identification purposes. The organisms must be carefully collected to prevent structural damage. Record the dimensions before the organism is killed. Only living specimens or those freshly killed should be used to determine color, since colors fade after death. Preservatives such as alcohol may drastically modify colors or bleach them. Keep subaquatic specimens wet, as their colors will fade as they dry. Likewise, determine the colors of surface insects from dry samples. (This same principle helps when selecting materials for the imitations: Materials for constructing wet flies should be wet when color selection is made, and materials for dry flies should be dry.)

Since trout see food organisms at very close range, color description should be made with the aid of a magnifying glass. A 10X hand lens often reveals startling subtleties in color not apparent to the naked eye. Gray wings may suddenly take on strong overtones of amber, giving the wings a dun color; yellow bodies may no longer appear yellow, but soft orange. In addition, the organism may be a combination of colors. Unless it is viewed with a lens, the colors will blend in the eye to form an overall impression of some-

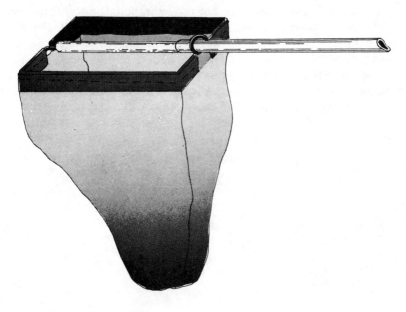

Fig. 2–4. Net for aerial insects

thing that's not really there. Great care should be used to overcome prejudices that could affect perception. Lighting is also critical in color perception. The human eye compares the brightness of an object to the brightness of the whole scene. Color is estimated in relationship to the general color of the scene. Although a black object in bright light actually reflects more light than a white object in dim light, the latter would appear brighter because of the averaging performed by the eye. Likewise, a yellow object in sunlight would appear green under blue light and orange under red light. As the available light decreases, colors tend to blend, diminishing in intensity until they are only shades of gray. Artificial lights often contain higher percentages of some wavelengths than sunlight, incandescent lamps more reds, and fluorescent lamps more blues. These excess amounts of certain wavelengths may slightly alter an object's color. But while specimens are best viewed in natural light, the use of artificial light cannot always be avoided. Very low intensities or monochromatic light, however, should be avoided since important colors in the organism may not be seen.

While there are many solutions that can be used to kill and preserve aquatic organisms, alcohol is the best. Rubbing alcohol works just fine. Use enough alcohol that the body juices of the organism do not dilute it greatly. An ounce of solution will preserve about a dozen medium-sized insects such as the Hendrickson. Keep the insects in tightly capped vials or other small bottles. For each organism, the date of capture, stream, section of stream (as accurately as possible), and collector should be noted on a small tag of paper inserted in the vial. Heavy white paper is best. Write the information on the tag with a number three or harder lead pencil (softer leads may smear and ink will dissolve from the paper).

In order to identify certain mayflies, you will need to collect the male spinners, recognized by the claspers on the terminal abdominal segment (fig. 2–5). These jointed, fingerlike appendages are used to hold the female

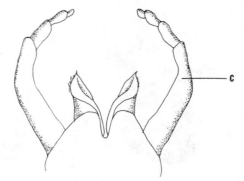

Fig. 2–5. Claspers (C) occur on terminal end of male insects.

Stream _____ Date _____

Section _____ No. _____

Water: H N LO   Time: m|,|,|,|,|,|,|,|,|,|,|,|,|,|,|n

Conditions: C Dk Mk Md

Bottom: M Mr Hp Sd G St Bd Br V

Current: S,M,F, □P □F

□RF □RN □RP □C

Air   Temp   H₂O   Time

Weather: Cl H S Cd O

D R Ts Sl Sn

Wind: C Lb Mb Sb Gl Gs

From: W Nw N Ne E Se S Sw

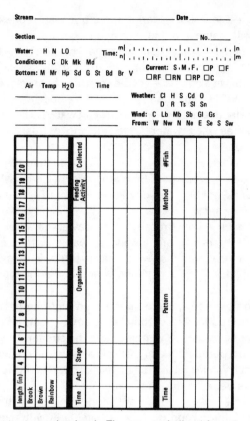

Fig. 2–6. Page from stream log book. The reverse is lined for notes and remarks.

during copulation. With a little observation, sexing individual insects is easy.

Information such as bottom type, current, and temperature is noted in the stream records. Through the years, these permanent notes can be winnowed, sorted, and correlated. Good records are invaluable, poor records useless, or worse yet, misleading. Recording must be accurate and the type of data consistent from trip to trip and year to year. Figure 2–6 is a page from the stream log used by Bob Pils and myself. Such information has figured heavily in our angling success through the years, allowing us to catalog the organisms of our streams, establish hatching sequences, and record experimental patterns, tackle, and memorabilia of angling.

Abbreviations on the notes are as follows:

Water: H — high, N — normal, L — low

Conditions: C — clear, Dk — dark (tannic bog water for example), Mk — milky (with some silt), Md — muddy

Bottom: M — mud, Mr — marl (shells mixed with silt), Hp — hardpan, Sd — sand, G — gravel (stones to grapefruit size), St — stony (stones to bushel basket size), Bd — boulders, Br — bedrock, V — vegetation

Current: S — slow, M — medium, F — fast, P — pool, F — flat (long area of uniform depth and flow with no broken water), Rf — riffles, Rn — run (narrow area where water is deep and moves briskly), Rp — rapids, C — cascade

Weather: Cl — clear, H — hazy, S — sunny (less than fifty percent cloud cover), Cd — cloudy (less than fifty percent clear sky), O — overcast (no clear sky visible), D — drizzle, R — rain, Ts — thunderstorm, Sl — sleet, Sn — snow

Wind: C — calm, Lb — light breeze (ruffles leaves and water surface), Mb — moderate breeze (branches move, water surface choppy), Sb — strong breeze (branches whip, waves form), Gl — gale (trees bend, whitecaps form), Gs — gusting winds of one of above categories

When taking field notes, use a number three or harder pencil.

Al Caucci and Bob Nastasi chronicle the day's events on a cassette tape recorder, dictating as they drive home from the stream. The tapes are later transcribed into a permanent diary. This is a useful technique, but valuable data can be lost if you forget to tape them. Keeping records on paper, as the events occur, is better in the long run.

Researching the biology of the trout's food organisms, the angler is confronted with scientific jargon and names. Familiarity with scientific names is helpful to the angler both because information on an organism may be listed under the scientific name and because local names can be confusing. Common names vary with locale, but scientific names are international. For example, Giant Michigan Mayfly, Michigan Caddis, Caddis, and The Mayfly are all local names for *Hexagenia limbata.* Scientific names and classification have acquired an unfair reputation of being enigmatic and difficult. The hierarchy of classification is merely a method for placing similar organisms into a group. For animals, the largest group is the kingdom Animalia. Based on structure and ancestry, each organism is placed into smaller groupings within the kingdom, until only those exactly like itself remain. Each of these successively smaller groups is given a name: phylum, class, order, family, genus, and species. A mnemonic device for remembering the sequence of these groups is: King Phillip Crossed Over From Germany Swimming.

Scientists often find that realignment of the classification scheme is necessary. Modern methods of tissue analysis and other techniques have led to a much better understanding of ancestral relationships. In addition, new species are discovered each year. Such realignment is not done lightly, and there are often disputes about proposed schemes. Stonefly classification, for example, is currently undergoing a massive upheaval with many proposals for realignment at the family and genus levels. Until a concensus is reached, the scheme last agreed upon takes preference. For this book, the standard references were: for the mayflies, *Mayflies of North and Central America* by Edmunds et al., 1976; for the caddises, *Larvae of the North American Caddisfly Genera* by Wiggins, 1977; for all other aquatic insects, *An Introduction to the Aquatic Insects of North America,* edited by Merritt and Cummins, 1978; for all terrestrial insects, *The Common Insects of North America* by Swan and Papp, 1972; for all noninsect invertebrates, *Freshwater Invertebrates of the United States* by Pennak, 1953; for fishes, *Fishes of the Great Lakes Region* by Hubbs and Lagler, 1958; for mammals, *Mammals of the Great Lakes Region* by Burt, 1957.

The scientific name of an organism is expressed as a genus and species. The names are in Latin since it is a dead language that will not change through common usage. The first letter of the genus is capitalized, the species is written in lowercase letters, and both are underlined or italicized. For example, the scientific name (binomial) for the Giant Michigan Mayfly is *Hexagenia limbata.* "Spp." means "species," and in phrases such as *"Tricorythodes* spp." stands for all or several species of a genus.

The species is the smallest category and is defined as a homogenous group of individuals forming a breeding population that in nature does not breed with any other group. There can be variation in size, color, and shape of individuals within the species. Arabian, Morgan, and thoroughbred horses readily cross breed and are thus members of the same species. This wide variation in individual horses has been produced by selective breeding procedures established by man, and in nature such wide diversity within a species is not usually found. However, regional differences in an insect species with respect to size, coloration, and hatching dates can occur and be significant to the angler. When fishing new waters, the knowledge of local anglers can be an invaluable aid in this regard.

For the angler's purpose, very few organisms need to be identified to the species level. The angler has to identify an organism to the level at which he can find information about its life history that will be applicable to his angling approach. How far the identification has to be carried depends upon the diversity of each taxonomic group to which the organism belongs and upon how much is known about the biology of the organism. If all the members of a taxonomic group have similar habits, occupy similar habitats, and have the same shape, it is not necessary to identify the organism beyond that level. If, however, the members of the group have extremely varying habits, habitats, life cycles, shapes, and so on, then the organism must be identified further. For curiosity's sake, you may wish to know the genus and species of a scud that occurs in your home waters, but simply knowing it's a scud (order Amphipoda) will lead you to all the information necessary to successfully fish an imitation. Knowing only that an organism is an insect (order Insecta) puts you a long way from any information of angling value. Even knowing that the insect is a mayfly, stonefly, or caddisfly is of little value for obtaining information. Mayflies, for example, are extremely variable in size, color, hatching dates, emergence characteristics, and other traits. Identifying the mayfly's family allows access to a great deal of biological information that can be applied to fishing strategies. Identification to the genus level will add further information. In some instances, even more might be added by identifying the species. Knowing that a mayfly is a Hendrickson *(Ephemerella subvaria)*, for example, opens the door to the writings of dozens of other anglers who have had experiences with this fly. But only a few organisms need to be keyed to the species level. Below is a list of the organisms discussed in this book and the taxonomic group to which I feel they need to be identified in order to gain maximum angling information.

Phylum: Arthropoda
  Class: Insecta
      Order: Ephemeroptera (mayflies) — identify to genus, occasionally to species
      Order: Plecoptera (stoneflies) — identify to family, occasionally to genus
      Order: Trichoptera (caddisflies) — identify to family, occasionally to genus
      Order: Diptera (midges and others) — identify to family
      Order: Odonata (dragonflies and damselflies) — identify to suborder, occasionally to family and genus
      Order: Hemiptera (bugs) — identify to family
      Order: Megaloptera (fishflies and others) — identify to family, occasionally to genus
      Order: Coleoptera (beetles) — for terrestrials, identify to order; for larvae of aquatic species, identify to family, occasionally to genus
      Order: Lepidoptera (moths) — identify to order
      Order: Hymenoptera (ants and others) — identify to order, occasionally to family
      Order: Orthoptera (grasshoppers and crickets) — identify to order
  Class: Crustacea — identify to order
Phylum: Annelida (worms and leeches) — identify to class

Phylum: Mollusca (snails and clams) — identify to class
Phylum: Cordata
  Class: Agnatha (lampreys) — identify to class
  Class: Osteichthyes (fish) — identify to family
  Class: Amphibia (frogs) — identify to class
  Class: Mammalia (mice) — identify to class

The keys and descriptions in the text are designed to carry the identification process to these recommended levels.

The angler can approach the actual keying process from several directions. Become familiar with the general shapes of the organisms; simply page through this book and look at the drawings. Then read the descriptive material in the keys and note sizes, colors, habitats, emergence dates, and so on. Often this alone will accurately identify an organism. The keys themselves are arranged in couplets. Always read both choices before deciding which is correct. For example, 1a might read "insect with filamentous tails" and 1b read "insect without tails or tails broad and paddleshaped." Reading only the first choice could be misleading without the information provided by the second choice. A number following a choice indicates the next couplet in the identification sequence. For each couplet, then, select the correct choice and proceed to the next, indicated couplet. In this way, the organism will eventually be identified.

3

Mayflies

Mayflies are the cornerstone of modern fly fishing. Throughout our angling heritage have ebbed and flowed the currents of devotion to these insects, upon whose ephemeral qualities the fly fisher has built a sport that endures through time. Dedication to fishing mayfly artificials has produced patterns as diverse in form and construction as they are vast in numbers, and many items of tackle have evolved from refining the techniques used to fish these patterns. The angling literature is rich with works inspired by these ethereal insects. To many the mayfly is an enchantress whose very name recalls soft spring days and sparkling streams.

To the entomologist, the mayflies are the order Ephemeroptera, *ephemo* for short-lived, *ptera* for wing, referring to the short life of the adults. Mayflies are broadly distributed in clean lakes and streams, and the adult forms of the over six hundred species of North America range from three to as much as forty millimeters in length. Metamorphosis of these insects is incomplete: from the egg hatches a nymph which eventually gives rise to the adult, the entire life cycle lasting from several months to as much as two years.

NYMPHS AND EMERGERS

Mayfly eggs have coiled, adhesive filaments or a jellylike coating, and once deposited in the water sink rapidly and stick to bottom structures. Eggs may hatch within a couple of weeks or may remain dormant over the winter and hatch the next spring. As the nymphs increase in size they shed their skins (molt) a number of times. Most species feed on vegetable detritus and microscopic organisms, chiefly diatoms; a very few species are omnivorous or predacious.

Consistent with the general body plan of insects, the nymph has a head, a thorax, and an abdomen. The head bears a pair of large, compound eyes, usually several simple eyes, and a pair of short antennae. The thorax consists of three segments; there is one pair of legs on each segment. Wing pads, containing the developing wings of the adult, are found on the middle and hind thoracic segments; however, the wing pads on the hind segment are small and usually covered by those of the middle segment. The abdomen consists of ten visible segments, and gills are borne on the upper surface or along the sides of some or all of the first seven segments. Mayfly nymphs have two or three tails. One visible pair of wing pads and gills along the abdomen distinguish mayfly nymphs from other immature aquatic insects.

Mayfly nymphs have four basic body plans which often reflect the habits of the particular species. Clinging nymphs (family Heptageniidae) inhabit strong currents and are markedly flat, allowing the insects to take advantage of the hydraulic cushion occurring at the surface of rocks, logs, and other bottom structures. The Quill Gordon *(Epeorus pleuralis,* fig. 3–1) and the March Brown *(Stenonema vicarium)* are classic clinging nymphs.

Burrowing nymphs occupy areas of slow to moderate flow; have strongly developed legs and large tusklike mandibles for digging; and bear large, filamentous gills. Waving the gills creates minute currents which constantly bring fresh, oxygenated water into the burrow. These insects are found in the families Ephemeridae and Polymitarcyidae, the Brown Drake *(Ephemera simulans,* fig. 3–2) and Giant Michigan Mayfly *(Hexagenia limbata)* being well-known examples.

Some nymphs are powerful swimmers, and although they usually crawl about or cling to objects, they often move by swimming. The families Baetidae, Siphlonuridae, and Metretopodidae contain these sleek, torpedo-shaped insects that readily dart about in currents of all velocities. The Leadwing Drake *(Isonychia bicolor,* fig. 3–3) and the Tiny Gray-Winged Olive *(Pseudocloeon anoka)* are examples.

Other nymphs crawl about, cling to objects, or sprawl in silt. They are awkward swimmers and in general have rounded, tapered bodies. Although found in all water types, they are most common in moderate to slow currents. The famous Hendrickson *(Ephemerella subvaria,* fig. 3–4) and Tiny White-Winged Black *(Tricorythodes* spp.) are examples. This category

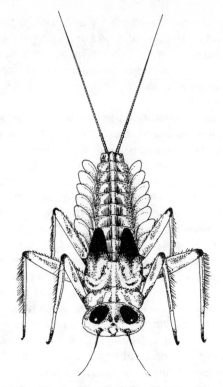

Fig. 3–1. Clinging mayfly nymph of the Quill Gordon *(Epeorus pleuralis)*

embraces the families Ephemerellidae, Leptophlebiidae, Caenidae, Tricorythidae, Baetiscidae, and Potamanthidae.

Mayfly nymphs are an important component of a biological phenomenon known as "drift," the downstream transport of aquatic or terrestrial organisms by stream currents. Although aquatic invertebrates (insects, crustaceans, and so on) have evolved mechanisms to help prevent being washed away, it is not unexpected that an occasional one will lose its foothold and be carried off. Such events occur randomly throughout the day. This low-level, but fairly continual transport is termed constant drift. Because of this consistent movement of organisms, trout are continually on the alert for food items in the currents. Nymph fishers capitalize on this phenomenon.

The scouring action of floods often causes wholesale displacement of the bottom fauna, called catastrophic drift. Other factors that can precipitate mass movement are drought, high stream temperature, anchor ice, and chemical pollutants. During high water periods, many invertebrates float free in the stream and trout gorge on the abundant fodder. During such times, concentrate your angling on the areas of the stream (eddies,

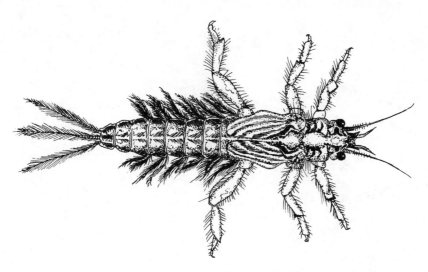

Fig. 3–2. Burrowing mayfly nymph of the Brown Drake *(Ephemera simulans)*

backwashes, insides of corners) where the drifting organisms settle out of the fast water. Ed Van Put, whose angling skills are legendary among eastern anglers, counts this as one of his most successful early season tactics (see "High-Water Trout" in *Rod and Reel* magazine, volume 1, number 2, 1979). If conditions become too severe, however, devastation of

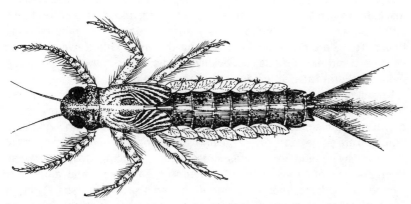

Fig. 3–3. Swimming mayfly nymph of the Leadwing Drake *(Isonychia bicolor)*

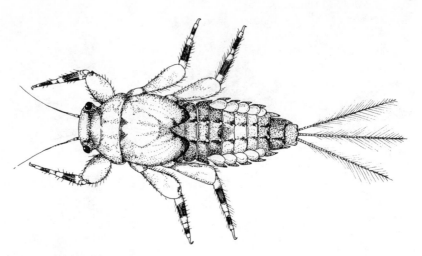

Fig. 3–4. Crawling mayfly nymph of the Hendrickson *(Ephemerella subvaria)*

the stream's invertebrate fauna can occur. Several years may pass before the organisms again reach fully stocked levels.

In recent years, researchers have found that some aquatic organisms drift in great abundance during one period of the twenty-four-hour day but not during other periods. For reasons not yet fully understood, but probably associated with population pressures or dispersal, many aquatic invertebrates leave the protective cover of the bottom and drift along in the currents. This behavioral drift includes thousands of individuals in small streams, millions in large rivers. The greatest peak in numbers of free-floating organisms occurs just after dark. Another, but smaller, peak occurs just before dawn. With such a large number of organisms in the currents, it's little wonder that fish forage actively in the evening and early morning hours. These are prime times for fishing the water with a nymph. Some species of drifting insects, especially caddis larvae, have their highest behavioral drift rates at midday rather than at night.

Not all mayflies, or all invertebrates for that matter, are involved in behavioral drift. The three most abundant organisms in the drift are the *Baetis* mayflies, some scuds, and some blackfly larvae. Also found in significant numbers are some caddisfly larvae and some stoneflies. Others involved in a minor way include water mites; cressbugs; aquatic beetles; water boatmen; backswimmers; larvae of dobsonflies, fishflies, and alderflies; nymphs of the damselflies and dragonflies; and dixa midge larvae. Rarely or never found in behavioral drift samples (but occurring in catastrophic and constant drift) are most burrowing insects, predatory forms, strong swimmers, fast water mayflies (Heptageniidae), caddis larvae that cement their cases to the bottom or build cases of large pebbles, mollusks, and most Diptera larvae. For a complete review of the scientific literature on drift, see Waters, 1972.

Flies should be fished dead drift to imitate the free-floating naturals. Patterns of coarse dubbing, fuzzy yarns, soft feathers, and so on are good because the materials of the fly move and simulate life even when fished dead drift. Jim Bashline's book *Night Fishing for Trout* is a must for the anglers who wish to fish the dark hour drift periods. Bashline recommends big, juicy wet flies, but nymphs such as the Muskrat, Red Brown, Strip Nymph, and Hair Leg Wooly Worm are also excellent.

The majority of the mayfly's life is spent as a nymph, and it is not until the next to the last instar that the adult begins to form within the nymphal shuck. During this development of the adult, the nymph does not feed, its mouth parts atrophy, and its wing pads become swollen and dark from the enlarging wings within (fig. 3–1). By checking the development of a nymph's wing pads, the angler can predict an imminent hatch.

The date and hour of the adult's emergence is specific for most species, as is the actual place of emergence. Nymphs of several genera climb out of

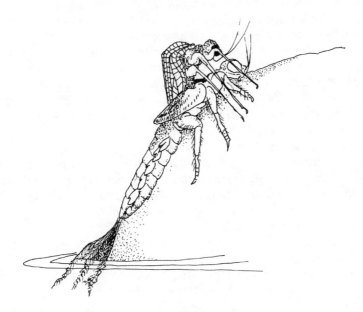

Fig. 3–5. Some mayflies crawl from the water before the adult emerges from the nymphal husk.

Fig. 3–6. A few mayfly adults emerge from the nymphal case while still underwater.

the water onto a stone or other object and emerge there (fig. 3–5). Once out of the water, the nymphs are not bothered by foraging trout, but large numbers of these insects are picked off during migration along the bottom. A nymph fished around stones, logs, bridge abutments, or other hatching sites during emergence periods is quite effective. In a few other genera, emergence of the adult takes place on the stream bottom (fig. 3–6) or as the nymph swims to the surface. A winged wet fly fished deep and twitched back to the surface can be a deadly imitation of these emerging insects.

In the majority of cases, the nymph rises to the surface and rides along in the film where emergence takes place (fig. 3–7); this process takes from a few seconds to as much as two minutes or more. The largest trout frequently remain beneath the surface, feeding on the rising nymphs or sucking the emerging insects out of the surface film. A nymph fished dead drift in the middle layers of the water or just beneath the surface serves very well in this case. An emerger pattern or spider-type wet fly can be very productive when the trout are feeding in the surface film.

The physical process of emergence is the same for all species. The thorax splits along the top and the adult pulls itself out of the nymphal shuck. The crumpled wings are the first structures to emerge through the split, followed by the thorax, head, and legs. Once this far, the insect perches on the surface film and withdraws its abdomen from the nymphal husk. Wings are sacklike extensions of the body wall, and the newly emerged adult must remain motionless until they are completely extended and hard. The insects

Fig. 3–7. Most mayfly adults emerge from the nymphal husk at the water's surface.

are quite vulnerable during this period and trout take them greedily — it is a time of joy and satisfaction for the dry fly angler.

The term emerger refers to the adult during the time of escape from the nymphal husk and before the wings are fully enlarged. In the normal sequence of hatching, the emerger first appears as a nymph with the crumpled adult wings sticking out between the shoulders. Then, as the adult frees itself, the emerger appears as half adult, half nymph (fig. 3–8). Some insects are unable to finish molting at this point and eventually drown. These have been called stillborns by Doug Swisher and Carl Richards. The last stage of the emerger sequence is the adult with unexpanded wings.

On any given stream the yearly rhythm of mayfly hatches is remarkably consistent. Once the angler has observed the sequence for his home waters, he can be confident that the hatches will occur in that series season after season. The exact date of the hatch varies and is partially controlled by annual weather fluctuations, but is predictable to within about a week. During cold years the hatch is delayed; in warm years the insects emerge

Fig. 3–8. A stillborn mayfly

early. The hour of the hatch is more consistent. Doug Swisher and Carl Richards described the timing very elegantly in *Selective Trout,* writing that the hatches occur during the most pleasant hours of the day: mid-afternoon in early spring, evening in late spring, morning and evening in summer, and back to mid-afternoon in fall. Caucci and Nastasi have correlated this phenomenon with water temperature: hatches generally occur when the water is between fifty and sixty-eight degrees Fahrenheit. In spring creeks or other consistently cold waters, insects hatch at cooler temperatures. The changes in daily cycles of air and water temperatures through the season result in the pattern described by Swisher and Richards. Because of temperature moderation on overcast days, evening hatches often occur earlier and morning hatches later than normal; both then last for a longer period. Armed with such information the angler can catalog the sequence of hatches on his waters by date and hour, an extremely important aid to successful angling.

Fishing imitations of immature aquatic insects had its genesis with the mayflies on the chalkstreams of England. There G. E. M. Skues studied the habits, structure, and coloration of nymphs and dressed the artificials that he fished so effectively. The modest collection of nymphs outlined in his *Nymph Fishing for Chalkstream Trout* includes exquisite examples of the fly dresser's art, and his basic pattern is the progenitor of modern imitations. The angling lessons offered in that text are as relevant today as they were provocative in those exclusive days of the dry fly.

Skues's patterns were tied with fur dubbing — still a favorite with many tiers — and showed concern for detail, manifested in attention to nymphal coloration, demarcation of abdomen and thorax, leg length, wing pads, and tails. But he confined himself to nymphing to individual fish in the period just prior to a hatch when the insects were near the surface. Since his day, new materials and tying procedures have evolved, and searching the water with a nymph has become a standard strategy. Pattern selection is not critical, as long as the imitation is generally representative of the insect life on the stream. For such tactics I rely on several patterns, favoring the Hair Leg Wooly Worm, various caddis pupae and larvae, the Muskrat Nymph, and several others, but especially the Red Brown Nymph (see fly patterns in the appendix).

Just prior to or during a hatch, however, trout can become highly selective, and to be effective, patterns must closely resemble the naturals. When a hatch is due, I switch to the correct pattern and fish the water until the hatch commences, then stalk individual fish in the time-honored manner of Skues.

Nymphing tactics should be geared to the particular type of water and organism. If the naturals are drifting deep along the bottom, fish the fly likewise. If there's a hatch in progress and trout are nymphing just under the film, the angler obviously wants to present the natural so it rides near the surface. Active nymphs should be aped with an actively worked fly; insects drifting motionless should be mimicked with a dead drift tactic. Various nymph fishing strategies are detailed in Charlie Brooks's *Nymph Fishing for Larger Trout* and in my book, *Nymphing.*

Nymph construction is a highly personal art, but when all the techniques are examined, a tying style emerges for each of the basic nymph types. For the large, very fuzzy looking, burrowing species, patterns should stress the gills and soft body of the natural. The Strip Nymph is excellent. The abdomen and gills are formed from a strip of tanned fur. Wing pads are formed of peacock herl and legs of cottontail rabbit guard hairs. Patterns with mohair or coarsely dubbed fur abdomens are also excellent.

Burrowing nymphs dig U-shaped burrows in the bottom where they should be safe from the trout. Such, however, is not the case, for during the molting period they leave their burrows and swim about until the skin is cast, returning to their holes with new exoskeletons. In addition, storms may wash them from the seclusion of their dens. Stomach samples have shown them to be available to the trout throughout the season. When emergence is near, the nymphs leave their burrows and quickly swim to the surface where the adult bursts the nymphal husk and emerges. The very largest trout work these hatches, feeding on the emerging nymphs and duns with splashing rises.

For the medium-sized swimming and crawling nymphs, I prefer the Red Brown Nymph design, using appropriately colored furs or yarns for the body — usually browns, tans, and olives. Since its inception in 1972, this pattern has accounted for more of my trout than any other single nymph imitation. It has taken large trout from the pastoral limestone streams of Pennsylvania to the expansive mountain rivers of the West and from the opening until the close of the season.

Clinging nymphs should be tied with a flat body, and many techniques have been offered to produce flat-bodied nymphs: dubbed fur soaked in lacquer and squeezed flat with pliers, cardboard forms tied on the hook, wire forms after the Ed Sisty fashion, and epoxy steel and hot glue molded on the shank. The most realistic method for tying convenience and overall effect was originated by George Grant of Butte, Montana. His flat-bodied flies are built on a foundation of brass straight pins cut to length and secured one on either side of the shank. The pointed ends of the pins are at the bend and the cut ends just behind the head. Copper, brass, or lead wire may also be used. I prefer lead wire since the thread bites into it slightly, producing an extremely rigid foundation. For unweighted flies, substitute limp monofilament for the wire.

Small nymphs — #16 through #28 — may be tied to show detail in structure; however, coloration and general configuration seem to be more important than exacting imitation. Frank Sawyer's Pheasant Tail nymph is an excellent illustration of this phenomenon. A river keeper on England's upper Avon, Sawyer has spent years closely observing nymphs and designing imitations; his observations and conclusions are carefully outlined in his fine book *Nymphs and the Trout.* The Pheasant Tail was tied to imitate the nymphs of the smaller species of the genus *Ephemerella.* It consists of little more than pheasant tail fibers wound on the hook, yet its success is undeniable. The dark rusty brown and black mottling of the tail fibers match the colors of the natural, and the finished shape of the nymph is impressively lifelike. Nymphs of many small species of mayflies are well imitated by the P.T., which has won this pattern an honored place in my fly boxes.

Another pattern that has proved effective for the small nymphs, especially #18 to #28, is the fur midge pupa described in *Selective Trout.* The fly is nothing more than dubbed fur — the abdomen of color to match the natural and tied thin, the thorax dark brown or black and tied full to suggest the robust thorax and dark wing pads of a mature nymph. For better penetration of the surface film, weight the fly under the thorax. This pattern imitates well almost all small insect life, including mayflies, midges, and caddisflies. It pays to carry a broad selection of these imitations.

In the hours prior to the hatch, fish the nymph, drifting it deep in the current or working it on the rising swing of the Leisenring lift. During the hatch, fish an emerger pattern, twitching it gently beneath the surface like the natural. Trout may be selecting duns or staying beneath the surface to capture the emergers. The real importance of the emerging insect was established by Doug Swisher and Carl Richards. Their painstakingly detailed observations on mayfly emergence clearly showed the emerger to be as important or more important than the dun in many cases. When dealing with large, deliberate fish, the emerger is certainly highly significant. Pay close attention to the feeding pattern before selecting your fly.

Emerger wings may be simulated with nylon stocking material, polypropylene yarn, maribou, or other materials tied in at the head and extending along the top of the fly to the rear of the thorax in the manner of a short, wet fly wing. Ted Rogowski developed the rolled nylon stocking wing; the history of this technique is outlined in Schwiebert's *Nymphs.* Roll a small square of gray nylon stocking (mesh is best) between the fingers to form a tight tube which is tied in and cut to length. The tube should be picked out with a bodkin, forming a fuzzy mass of fibers that beautifully matches the unfurling wing of the natural. A piece of gray poly yarn (see dyeing instructions in the appendix) may also be used to form this emerger wing. It is more buoyant than the nyon material and is excellent for emerger patterns to be fished in the film. The new sparkle yarns make a most effective emerger wing, also. In any case, care must be taken when cutting the wing to length. These materials stretch slightly, and if pulled taut before being trimmed, will snap back disappointingly short.

René and Bonnie Harrop of Saint Anthony, Idaho, are well known for the fly patterns they have created to fool the sophisticated rainbows of Henry's Fork. These flies are based on sound entomological observations. Their dry nymph pattern is a good example; it imitates the adult with unexpanded wings. The body is the same color as the adult, and a rolled clump of dubbing simulates the unfurled wings. During a hatch, the fly is fished dry and is often more successful than nymph or dun imitations.

Stillborn patterns are tied to represent an emerger that has not completely shed its nymphal case. A tail of deer hair, hackle points, ostrich herl, or other material imitates the partially cast case. The body should be the same color as the adult, and wings should be tied short (emerger style). This theory applies to all insects that emerge in the surface film. These imitations can be the secret to taking particularly selective fish. The stillborn concept and patterns are nicely detailed in *Fly Fishing Strategy.*

The Quill Gordon and several others emerge on the bottom and swim to the surface as an adult. The nymphs line up on the downstream edges of rocks in fast current and transform. As they struggle to reach the surface, the duns are carried swiftly downstream to pools and pockets of slower water where they finally bob to the top. In such places, good numbers of fish will take a weighted emerger or a wet fly dressed to represent the adult.

Adults of many of the species in the family Ephemerellidae emerge from the nymphal skin while still submerged. For the larger species of these flies, the nylon stocking, poly yarn, or sparkle yarn emergers and stillborns are excellent. Another pattern that has proved especially valuable is a spider-type fly as described by Ray Ovington in *How to Take Trout on Wet Flies and Nymphs.* These flies are dressed on #10 to #24 and consist merely of an unwaxed, silk thread or dubbed body and a soft bird hackle wound at the head. To be most effective, the hackle should come from the shoulder of the bird's wing (covert feathers). The fibers of these feathers are broad yet soft, unlike the thin fibered body feathers. A broad fiber gives the fly needed form and permits floatation. To fish the fly in the film, lightly coat the hackle with floatant. If the fish refuse the pattern in the film, pull it sharply to sink it, then retrieve the fly slowly just beneath the surface.

Because this pattern is fished wet or dry, it's been named the Wet/Dry Fly. Its rumpled appearance suits it for many angling situations: fished dry as emerger or stillborn, fished dry with action to imitate fluttering duns and so on, fished wet to simulate dead drifting pupae or emergers, twitched just under the surface to imitate active emergers, fished on the rising swing of the Leisenring lift, and so forth. So versatile is this pattern that my fly boxes contain dozens in many colors and sizes. Covert feathers from mallard, grouse, crow, starling, woodcock, and other birds can be used in the Wet/Dry Fly. The most used color combinations are slate (coot) /olive, gray (mallard) /yellow, grouse/tan, slate/rusty brown, and black (crow) /gray. Often when a more perfectly tied pattern does not succeed, one of these crumpled, simple little flies will turn the trick. The silhouette is representative of so many insects that every angler should carry a few and give them an honest try.

DUNS

The adult that emerges from the nymphal shuck is known as the sub-imago or dun and is usually drab in color and clothed in minute hairs, and has dark colored wings. Occasionally, as with the Hendrickson and Tiny White-Winged Black, the male and female have different coloration. Most species have two pairs of wings, although the hind wings are greatly reduced and not often noticeable. The very small mayflies of Caenidae and Tricorythidae and some Baetidae have only one pair of wings. At rest the adult holds its wings upright over its back, a characteristic that is unique among the aquatic insects and one that has prompted anglers to liken them to miniature sailboats (fig. 3–9). In the very tiny mayflies (three to five millimeters) the wing is a little longer than the body. In the medium-sized adults (six to twenty millimeters), the wing and body are the same length. In the big duns and spinners (twenty to forty millimeters), the wing is a little shorter than the body.

Trout feed readily, often greedily, on the newly emerged duns, and a hatch of big mayflies such as the Giant Michigan Mayfly will stimulate the largest trout to feed recklessly at the surface. Dry fly fishing is an exciting and productive method during such times.

Modern dry fly construction was radically changed with the publication of Swisher and Richards's revealing *Selective Trout.* Their book stimulated a zealous search for new materials and techniques from which has emerged a veritable flood of new information and a revival of interest in techniques of the old masters. Several of their patterns nicely filled obvious gaps in my own boxes. Most wanting was a consistently successful imitation of the large duns. The success of conventional patterns had waxed and waned with the whims of the trout and fishing conditions, but Swisher and Richards's deer hair, Extended-Body Para-Drake has been a remarkably consistent producer. This pattern makes easy the once difficult task of imitating such insects as the Giant Michigan Mayfly, the Brown Drake, and other large duns.

Fig. 3–9. Mayfly duns sit on the water with wings upright, giving the appearance of tiny sailboats.

The hollow deer-body hair adds greatly to its buoyance, but for maximum floatation, coat the body and hackle with a paste fly dressing such as Muclin or Gink. The fly will then ride on the film like the natural, rather than partially submerged in the film.

Fish take these large flies very positively and the angler is tempted to strike quickly — don't. Hesitate long enough for the fish to close his mouth on the fly, and then pull the hook home. A short strike in the case of these large flies is most often a fast strike by the angler, not a miss by the fish.

During a heavy hatch, the fly must be presented accurately with casts timed to the rises of the trout. If the fish constantly refuses the fly, even when all else seems correct, try hitting him on the head to get his attention. When you see the trout rise, immediately cast the fly to the ring. Often the fish quickly turns and grabs the artificial, so be prepared.

For that period of the season when these large flies are hatching, the trout acquire "pattern and color hangovers" and are constantly on the alert for the big duns. Early morning fishing after a heavy hatch can be surprisingly effective, the big Para-Drake often pulling up the largest trout in the stream. Wade cautiously and watch closely, for the trout are not sequestered in deep holes, but cruising actively in search of food.

Many techniques will simulate the medium-sized mayflies. The Variant, the Poly-Dun, Swisher and Richards's Cut-Wing Para-Drake and No-Hackle

Duns, and Caucci and Nastasi's Compara-Dun are the patterns most in vogue.

The Variant is an excellent broken water pattern that can take much abuse. The tail should be of stiff hackle fibers or guard hairs. For the body, use dubbing and treat it with a paste dressing. The hackle should be the color of the natural's wings. No other wings are used on the Variant. Good quality hackle should be used. For an excellent discussion of hackle feathers, see Howard West's chapter in *The Second Fly Tyer's Almanac* edited by Boyle and Whitlock. During emergence, duns often flutter on the surface in an attempt to get airborne or as they struggle to leave the nymphal husk. A Variant fished with an occasional twitch is a fine representation under these conditions. Cast the fly and let it sit still for a couple of seconds, then give it a small twitch, let it rest, and so on. Another advantage of the Variant is that trimming the hackle top and bottom converts it into a fine spinner imitation.

The other patterns are all fine for highly selective trout in smooth or broken water. Their silhouettes are very realistic and they withstand a good deal of abuse before they need to be steamed to return them to their original condition. Like the big Extended-Body Para-Drakes these flies should be treated with paste floatant to assure that they sit on, not in, the surface film. For an upright wing fly, the Poly-Dun is very good. The tails are stiff hackle fibers or guard hairs split to form a wide V. The body is dubbed. Form a single, upright wing with poly or sparkle yarn. The hackle is wound parachute style.

The No-Hackle Duns have a split tail, dubbed body, and duck quill wings tied in at the sides of the thorax. The secrets to successfully tying these flies are good stiff hackle fibers for the tail, tying the wings in at the sides rather than on the top of the fly (the wings will form a V when viewed from the front and help support the fly on the water), and lacquering the basal one-third of the wings with vinyl cement to prevent their splitting. For more specific diagrams and detailed instructions see Swisher and Richards's *Selective Trout* and *Fly Fishing Strategy*.

Caucci and Nastasi's Compara-Dun is tied with split tail, dubbed body, and wing of deer hair taken from the animal's face. The wing is tied in as for the big Extended-Body Para-Drakes, but allowed to flare so that the outer hairs of the wing stick out to the sides and act as outriggers. *Hatches* gives a good selection of Compara-Duns for mayflies.

These patterns show some of the variations in techniques that have resulted in effective imitations. They are a reminder that the angler should be flexible in thought and action. I use the Variant and Poly-Dun, but each angler should select those flies he feels most comfortable tying and fishing. A fisherman's confidence in his patterns is important!

For the small mayfly duns, the details of the wing and body are critical, especially for selective trout in smooth currents. Experimentation has led me to adopt a modified version of Andy Puyan's Loop-Wing for small flies (#20 to #28). This technique produces a beautiful, obvious wing on the smaller flies. The loop wing is not totally suitable for the larger flies since it causes them to spin and twist the leader when cast.

The tiny duns offer some unique fishing. When the trout are actively feeding on these insects, they often lose their usual sense of caution but become extremely selective and will not move more than several inches in the feeding lane to take a fly. By carefully stalking each fish and accurately presenting the fly on a short line, the chances of hooking the fish are excellent. Like the Para-Drakes on the other end of the size spectrum, these minute Loop-Wings require a pause after the trout takes the fly. Wait until the trout turns down before gently pulling the hook home. If this is properly executed, the fly will hang in the tongue or the fleshy part of the jaw and not pull away. Bending the point of the hook slightly to one side will increase its chances of catching a good hold.

SPINNERS

After the dun's wings have fully dried, it flutters to streamside vegetation and begins a period of rest that may last from several moments to several days. During this time the insect does not feed; its mouthparts have atrophied. Cold or wet weather extends this spell by a day or two. Mayflies are the only insect with two winged adult stages. At the conclusion of the inactive period, the thorax of the dun splits down the back and the second adult stage emerges. This adult is the imago or spinner, and is the sexually mature stage. The spinner usually has a glossy body with clear wings; has larger eyes, longer tails, and forelegs; and may be a completely different color than the dun. In the diminutive species of the genera *Brachycerus, Caenis,* and *Tricorythodes* and the larger *Ephoron,* transformation from dun to spinner occurs only a few minutes after the dun emerges from the nymphal skin. Shedding of the dun's coat is often not complete before these impatient spinners take wing. Then, as the insects fly over the water, the skins are finally shed, forming delicate clouds as they fall. This has led some people to mistakenly assume that the spinners shed their dun skins totally while in flight.

Although it's possible to tell males from females in the dun stage, it's much easier to separate him from her in the spinner stage. In all families except Caenidae and Tricorythidae the eyes of the male are very large. In some species the top of the male's eyes may be brightly colored; in some a distinctly colored band separates the top and bottom portions of the eye. The forelegs of males are much longer than those of the females and bend

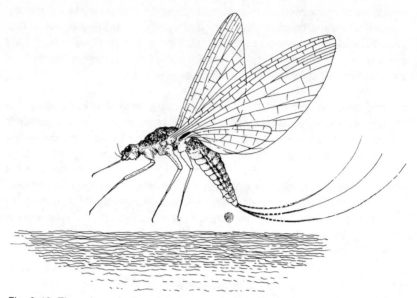

Fig. 3–10. The spinner is the sexually mature adult stage of the mayfly.

downward and upward. The large eyes and reversible forelegs are adaptations for mating. The male flies underneath the female during copulation, reaching up and holding her with his forelegs.

Mating flights occur at various times of the day, depending on the season. Like emergence of the duns, spinner fall is temperature dependent, generally coming when the air is sixty to seventy degrees. The males gather in large numbers near or over the water and perform the nuptial dance. Many species rise and fall in graceful rhythm; others may simply fly about over the water. Females fly into the dancing swarm and select a mate, the pair coupling over the water or returning to land before mating. The male dies shortly after mating, falling onto the land or the water, and the gravid female deposits her eggs (fig. 3–10) and dies. The eggs sink rapidly and adhere to the bottom. During mating and egg laying, the spinners often fly a short way upstream to compensate for the downstream drift of the nymphs during the hatch.

When designing spinner imitations, the habits of the natural must be considered. Members of the family Baetidae crawl beneath the surface to oviposit directly on bottom structures. During spinner falls of these insects, females have even deposited eggs on the subsurface portion of my waders. After egg laying, the female dies and is carried away in the currents to become fodder for the trout. The Wet/Dry Fly or a winged wet fly can be very effective during such situations. Fish it dead drift with an occasional twitch.

In many species the females simply dip their abdomens into the water. Others drop onto the water and remain there for several seconds as they extrude some of their eggs, then rise into the air to dance for a period before laying more eggs. While the insects are on the water, their wings are held upright, and like the emerging duns they may flutter on the surface. Full-hackled flies such as the Variant can be twitched and skipped to imitate this activity. When all the eggs have been deposited, the females drop to the water and die. The wings relax and fall out to the sides (fig. 3–11). The spinner is then said to be spent. In some species the females simply drop onto the surface and remain there, extruding the eggs and twitching in their death throes. These, too, assume the spent configuration. The body and wings are flat on the surface forming a delicate cross. Trout lock in on this surface form and will refuse all objects of improper color and shape. Such hyperselectivity can be overcome if the artificial closely matches the color, dimensions, and shape of the natural. Vince Marinaro most expertly discusses the requirements for a good spinner imitation in his book *In the Ring of the Rise.*

For the small species, the Poly-Spinner is a remarkably effective pattern. The polypropylene yarn of its wings not only increases the fly's buoyance but is translucent and filmy like a spinner's wings. Perfectly hyaline wings are best imitated by white poly yarn; those with some translucency are effectively matched with off-white, light gray, or tan yarn. In other instances where the wings are a definite color, the yarn should be dyed to match the natural.

The yarn is laid crossways to the shank and secured with figure-eight wraps of thread. Head cement is applied to the base of each wing. Wings tied in this manner will be fully spent. In some species the hen may drop only

Fig. 3–11. A spent spinner

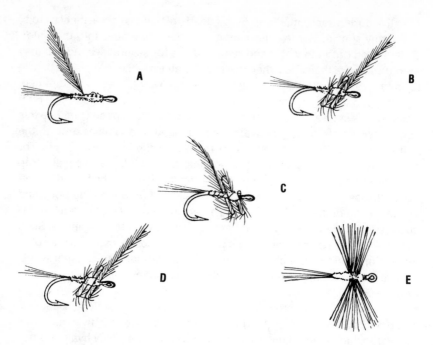

Fig. 3–12. Wrapping hackle in a figure-eight fashion. (A) Tie in hackle at rear of thorax. (B) Wrap hackle forward in two turns to head of fly. (C) Wrap two turns back over thorax. (D) Wrap forward to head. (E) Trim hackle top and bottom.

one wing to the surface. Imitation of these species requires that the wings be tied semi-spent, each wing tilted upward about thirty degrees from the horizontal. Fortunately the trout will often take fully spent flies when the naturals are semi-spent. If the artificial is refused, the dot of head cement at the wing bases allows the angler to force the wings upward into a semi-spent position.

Like all materials, polypropylene has limitations. On hooks larger than #16, it does not form a desirable spinner wing. Not only does poly yarn lack the necessary rigidity, but its bulk produces significant drag, causing the fly to become a spinner of a different sort, twisting the leader and line. Good quality hackle, trimmed top and bottom, produces a realistic silhouette while greatly reducing air resistance on spinners tied on #8 to #16. The tail is hackle fibers or guard hairs; the body may be the extended type or simply of dubbed fur. Hackle for the wings should be wound forward over the thorax in two open turns then rearward crossing these open turns with two more, then forward again (fig. 3–12). This double figure eight forces the hackle out into the desired wing shape and adds stiffness. Once wound, the hackle is trimmed top and bottom, and a drop of head cement is applied to the thorax.

For the very large mayflies, poly yarn and hackle fibers are too soft to form good spinner wings, so I use calf tail hair. An extended deer-hair body is formed and calf tail hair tied in pointing forward over the eye. The hair is split into two equal parts and the thread wrapped figure-eight style across these wings to pull them out into position. Finish the fly at the thorax and apply head cement at the wing bases.

In all cases, proper floatation and meniscus form are absolutely critical. This is the reason for using poly yarn, trimmed hackle, or hair wings rather than sheets of plastic or hackle points. The filaments in the yarn, hackle, or hair wings trap air and aid in buoying the fly, but more importantly, these materials give the same surface impression (when viewed from underwater) as do the veined and slightly corrugated wings of the natural. Wings of plastic, hackle points, or other sheetlike materials cannot give the correct surface impression. Vince Marinaro has documented this phenomenon in a series of fine color photos in his book, *In the Ring of the Rise.* To assure correct flotation and surface form of a fly once you've caught a fish on it, wash it off, dry it thoroughly, and reapply dressing if necessary.

Trout take spinners with a deliberate head and tail rise, gently porpoising as they suck in the spent flies. Because the spinners have such a low profile, the angler may overlook them entirely and fitfully ply the water with all manner of imitations in a futile effort to hit upon the right fly. A few minutes spent observing the water surface and collecting specimens with a hand sieve can spell the difference between the delights of fishing the spinner fall and the frustrations of guess and by gosh.

Spinners falling on a broken surface are often drowned and carried into the midwater depths. Trout will feed on these insects just as readily as they will feed at the surface. If spinners are falling in a riffle, for example, trout in the pool downstream will be feeding on the submerged insects. Fish your pattern wet at the head of the pool, twitching it occasionally.

As with the duns, the morning after a heavy spinner fall can be extremely productive. Be cautious and watch for cruising trout that are feeding with deliberate head and tail rises. Spinners caught in a spider's web or lying awash in the slow water along the bank are an indication that good, early morning spinner fishing could be waiting for the knowledgeable angler.

Since mayflies are first in the hearts of most fly fishers, much has been written about them. However, there are several texts that are of special significance. Ernie Schwiebert's *Matching the Hatch,* published in 1955, is a milestone in angling literature. So thoroughly did Schwiebert, then barely out of his teens, describe the major mayfly hatches of the United States that the book is still in print and highly regarded for its solid information. The most complete angling work on mayfly nymphs is Schwiebert's magnificent *Nymphs.* It is a resource book of startling magnitude and richness that describes not only the immature forms of mayflies but all the other important subaquatic forms. Schwiebert's magnum opus, *Trout,* the single most comprehensive treatise ever written on fly fishing, contains a section on angling entomology that very nicely details the natural history of mayflies and other food organisms. Habits and structure of most mayflies are described in Al Caucci and Bob Nastasi's *Hatches.* Not only are the nymphs, duns, and spinners authoritatively discussed and illustrated in an easily understood text, but the observations on fishing tactics are valuable to neophyte and experienced angler alike. The standard scientific reference is *The Mayflies of North and Central America* by Edmunds et al.

MAYFLY FAMILIES

These synopses include insects known to have fishable hatches. Not all mayflies are included in these synopses. Those insects that are confined to warm waters and those that occur very rarely have been omitted.

Family Baetidae; genera *Baetis, Callibaetis, Centroptilium, Cloeon, Pseudocloeon:* For most species, the nymphs overwinter, growing slowly in the icy water. Adults emerge in the spring and lay eggs that hatch immediately. The summer generation emerges in the fall and lays eggs that produce the overwintering generation. *Baetis vagans* and related species have three generations every two years. *Baetis* nymphs occur in lakes and slow to very rapid streams in shallow water where they cling or crawl about on vegetation, debris, gravel, or rocks. They feed on algae or detritus and can swim quite well. *Callibaetis* nymphs are pond and lake dwellers that occasionally occur in slow streams. They crawl or swim actively in vegetated areas and feed on algae and detritus. *Centroptilium* nymphs inhabit slow to moderate currents of spring creeks where they cling or crawl about on vegetation or rocks. They feed on algae or detritus and swim strongly. *Cloeon* nymphs prefer the slow waters of ponds, lakes, meadow streams, and edges of fast water streams. They crawl about on vegetation, feeding on algae, and can swim quite well. *Pseudocloeon* nymphs dwell in shallow riffles and fast water areas in streams and at lake edges where there is wave action. They feed on algae and move about by crawling or swimming strongly. All the Baetidae emerge at the film. Smaller species may have difficulty breaking through the surface film in smooth-flowing areas, so they emerge in choppy water where surface tension is lowered by the turbulent currents. Duns molt in a few hours: *Baetis* seven to twelve, *Callibaetis* seven to nine, *Centroptilium* ten to twelve, *Cloeon* six to seven, *Pseudocloeon* eight to ten. *Baetis* spinners crawl beneath the surface to lay eggs; the other genera drop to the surface and remain there while extruding the eggs. *Baetis, Callibaetis,* and *Pseudocloeon* are encountered most often and produce superhatches.

Family Baetiscidae; genus *Baetisca:* The humpbacked nymphs emerge from the eggs in summer and begin their growth. They do not grow during the winter, but resume growth in spring. Adults emerge in spring; there is one generation per year. These insects inhabit gravel riffles in streams or lake edges where there is wave action. They eat vegetation and detritus. Sprawlers, they can swim quite well. The nymphs crawl out of the water before the dun emerges. Spinners appear twenty-four to forty-eight hours later. This genus is not often encountered.

Family Caenidae; genera *Brachycerus, Caenis:* There are two generations per year in this family. Eggs are deposited in the fall and nymphs grow slowly over the winter. This generation hatches in the spring and lays eggs. These hatch and the second generation develops and emerges in late summer. The eggs of this second generation produce the overwintering nymphs. Nymphs of *Brachycerus* occur at the edges of streams and lakes. They sprawl in sand covered with a fine layer of silt. *Caenis* nymphs are largely pond and lake dwellers but do occur occasionally in slow streams. They sprawl in vegetation, debris, or silt. Both genera are poor swimmers and feed on algae and detritus. Emergence occurs at the film in the afternoon or at night. Duns alight and molt five to six minutes after emerging. Spinners may finish casting the dun shuck while in flight. In both genera, the spinners fall to the water to oviposit. These genera are common and can produce superhatches.

Family Ephemerellidae; genus *Ephemerella:* This is a very large and diverse genus. In most species, eggs hatch in the fall and the nymphs grow during the winter. Emergence occurs in spring or summer. In some species the nymphs may hibernate during the winter and resume growth in the spring. There is one generation per year. Although these omnivorous nymphs inhabit all water types and are found in vegetation, gravel, or debris, each species requires a specific current and substrate. Fast water species have large, flattened gills that they use like suction cups to hold fast to stones; slower water species hide in crevices or crawl about. All are moderately good swimmers. Duns of a few species emerge on the bottom or crawl out to emerge; most emerge as the nymph struggles to the surface or as it floats at the film. Transformation to the spinner stage occurs twenty-two to thirty hours after the duns emerge. Only one, large egg mass is deposited, released by touching the abdomen to the surface. This is one of the most important genera; it produces several superhatches.

Family Ephemeridae; genera *Ephemera, Hexagenia:* These are our largest mayflies. The nymphs are true burrowers, digging U-shaped tunnels in the bottom. Nymphs hatch in the summer and hibernate over the winter. Growth is completed in the spring. In the northern reaches of their range (Canada), *Hexagenia* nymphs require two years to develop. Both genera inhabit lakes and slow areas of streams, but *Ephemera* nymphs prefer fine gravel and silty sand while *Hexagenia* prefer firm silt. *Ephemera* nymphs may be carnivores or herbivores; hex nymphs are filter feeders that prefer algae and detritus. Both genera are surprisingly agile swimmers. Emergence occurs at the film in the evening or at night. Spinners appear twenty-four to forty-eight hours later and fall to the surface to oviposit. They twitch enticingly as the twin egg packets are being released. These widespread genera produce superhatches.

Family Heptageniidae; genera *Cinygma, Cinygmula, Epeorus, Heptagenia, Rhithrogena, Stenonema:* Species of *Cinygmula, Epeorus,* and *Rhithrogena* produce one generation per year. Eggs hatch in the fall and nymphs grow slowly over the winter. Adults emerge the following spring and summer. Exact details of the life histories of *Cinygma, Heptagenia,* and *Stenonema* are not certain, but they appear to produce only one generation per year. Emergence occurs during all the warm months. All Heptageniidae nymphs are very flat, clinging, and found in swift water. They feed on detritus and algae. All are poor swimmers. The *Cinygmula* are one of the most common mayflies of the western mountain streams and high lakes. In some streams they are a frequent component of behavioral drift. *Cinygma* are less frequent inhabitants of streams in the Sierra Nevadas. The large, oval gills of the *Epeorus* and *Rhithrogena* nymphs help them cling tenaciously to stones in shallow to moderately deep rapids. *Heptagenia* nymphs prefer the near-bank shallows of rapids and wave-washed beaches of lakes where they hide under rocks. *Stenonema* nymphs often wedge themselves into crevices among the rocks in rapids, but some species prefer plants and debris near shore. Others like lake edges where waves wash in. When mature, *Epeorus* nymphs crawl to the downstream edge of submerged rocks and emerge. The adults then swim to the surface. *Heptagenia* duns emerge underwater or at the film. *Cinygma, Cinygmula, Rhithrogena,* and *Stenonema* emerge at the film. The nymphs often migrate to the shallows near shore just before emergence. Duns molt approximately twenty to forty-eight hours after emergence. Spinners oviposit by dipping their abdomens or dropping to the surface repeatedly. *Cinygmula, Epeorus, Hep-*

tagenia, and *Stenonema* are most often encountered; they can produce superhatches.

Family Leptophlebiidae; genera *Leptophlebia, Paraleptophlebia:* The nymphs of *Leptophlebia* overwinter in a dormant state and complete their growth the next spring and summer. *Paraleptophlebia* overwinters in the egg stage and the nymphs grow rapidly in the next spring and summer. Both genera have only one generation per year. *Leptophlebia* nymphs like the vegetation and debris in lakes or quiet eddies near stream banks. These herbivores are crawlers, but can swim fairly well. The *Paraleptophlebia* occur in slow to rather swift currents in streams and live in gravel, debris, and vegetation where they crawl about feeding on algae and detritus. They are awkward swimmers. Mature *Leptophlebia* nymphs crawl and swim in schools to temporary springtime pools and marshes before the duns emerge. They will even cross dry ground to reach such areas. Emergence occurs at the film or on a wet mudbank in the marshes. Mature *Paraleptophlebia* nymphs migrate shoreward to quiet water areas. Some emerge in the film, many crawl from the water before emergence occurs. *Leptophlebia* duns molt eighteen to twenty-nine hours after emergence; *Paraleptophlebia* duns molt within twelve to forty-eight hours. Both genera deposit eggs by repeatedly dipping their abdomens in the water. *Leptophlebia* are locally important and produce good spinner falls. *Paraleptophlebia* are widespread and can produce superhatches.

Family Metretopodidae; genus *Siphloplecton:* Details of the life history of these insects are not known. Nymphs occur in lakes and slow to moderately flowing streams where they crawl about in gravel and vegetation. They are also active and powerful swimmers. The nymphs crawl from the water before the duns emerge; occasionally they are seen emerging in the film. Duns emerge in spring or early summer and molt in about forty-eight hours; the spinners are powerful fliers and drop their eggs while flying four to eight feet above the surface. Once in a while they fall to the water before extruding their eggs. This species is encountered infrequently.

Family Polymitarcyidae; genus *Ephoron:* Eggs of this genus do not hatch until the spring following their deposition. Nymphs grow rapidly and duns emerge in late summer and early fall. There is one generation per year. The nymphs burrow in sand, gravel, silt, or clay in the shallows of lakes and slow to swift streams. They feed on algae and detritus. Duns may emerge at the film or the nymphs may crawl out onto wet mud and sand before the duns hatch. The male molts immediately, but the cast dun husk often remains attached to the spinner's tails, giving the appearance of a greatly elongated insect. Females do not molt, but remain as duns. They settle to the surface to lay eggs. Hatching and egg laying occur just at dark and are completed in about an hour. Usually encountered in the warmer water stretches of trout streams (downstream reaches), they produce superhatches.

Family Potamanthidae; *genus Potamanthus:* This genus probably has one generation per year, but the details are not certain. Physically, these nymphs appear to be burrowers, but in reality they do not form true burrows. They sprawl or dig a shallow depression in silt, sand, or gravel in the eddies of swift, shallow areas or in other quiet areas of streams and feed on algae and detritus. They can swim well. Emergence is generally in the evening. The nymphs swim to the film where the duns emerge. Molting to the spinner probably occurs twenty-four to forty-eight hours later. The females fall to the film to oviposit and often twitch erratically as they release their eggs. Widespread and common in the East and Midwest, they produce good hatches.

Family Siphlonuridae; genera *Siphlonurus, Isonychia:* Eggs overwinter; nymphs hatch in spring and grow rapidly, emerging that spring or summer. There is one generation per year except for the Western Gray Drake *(Siphlonurus occidentalis),* which has two broods per summer. *Siphlonurus* nymphs are omnivores that live on the bottom or in vegetation in quiet water at stream edges. They are climbers but can swim rapidly. *Isonychia* nymphs are omnivores that cling to vegetation, debris, or rocks in fast currents. They use their hairy forelegs to strain the currents for food and are strong swimmers. All Siphlonuridae nymphs crawl from the water before the adults emerge. Occasionally, however, the *Isonychia* may emerge in the film. Duns of *Siphlonurus* transform to the spinner twenty-six to fifty-three hours after emergence from the nymphal husk. The *Isonychia* duns transform in twenty-two to thirty-one hours. All spinners in this family deposit eggs by repeatedly dipping the abdomen in the water. Widespread and common, they can produce super spinner-falls.

Family Tricorythidae; genus *Tricorythodes:* The eggs of these minute mayflies hatch in the spring. Two generations develop in sequence over the summer. Nymphs within the same generation develop at different rates, so although there are two peaks of emergence (midsummer and early fall), there are duns emerging continuously after midsummer. The tiny nymphs prefer slow eddies in fast water or other slow water areas where they sprawl in fine gravel and vegetation. They are awkward swimmers and feed on algae and detritus. Most species emerge in the morning, the nymph swimming to the film. Transformation to the spinner occurs from several minutes to two hours after the duns hatch. Some species appear to transform in flight, but this is not the case. Actually they land to molt, but the spinner takes wing before the dun's shuck is entirely cast off. It is then lost as the spinner dances over the water. *Tricorythodes atratus* (a midwest species) emerges underwater; males hatch in the evening and females hatch the following morning. Transformation to the spinner occurs in the morning for both males and females. Gravid females of all species fall to the surface and lay there as they extrude their egg packets. Widespread and common, they produce superhatches.

Keys to Mayflies

Nymphs

1a. Abdomen soft and fleshy, often tan; gills very large and feathery; legs broad and flanged for digging; tusks present (fig. 3–2): burrowing nymphs . . . I

1b. Not as above . . . 2

2a. Body strongly flattened; eyes located entirely on top of head; gills oval and conspicuous on abdominal segments one to seven (fig. 3–1): clinging nymphs . . . II

2b. Body not strongly flattened; eyes located at sides of head; gills variable (figs. 3–3, 3–4): swimming and crawling nymphs . . . III

I Burrowing nymphs

1a. Frontal prominence (on foremargin of head between antennae) extended and notched; tusks curved out (fig. 3–2): family Ephemeridae, genus *Ephemera*

1b. Frontal prominence smoothly rounded . . . 2

2a. Tusks curved up; very large nymphs burrowing in silt: family Ephemeridae, genus *Hexagenia*

2b. Tusks not as above . . . 3

3a. Tusks look distinctly like horns, legs broadly flattened (fig. 3–13); in gravel: family Potamanthidae, genus *Potamanthus*

3b. Tusks curved in with many bumps and hairs; frontal prominence slightly extended (fig. 3–14): family Polymitarcyidae, genus *Ephoron*

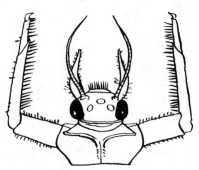

Fig. 3–13. Head of *Potamanthus* mayfly nymph

Fig. 3–14. Head of *Ephoron* mayfly nymph

II Clinging nymphs — all in the family Heptageniidae

1a. Two tails: genus *Epeorus*
1b. Three tails . . . 2

2a. Gills one and seven suction-cup-shaped and much larger than other gills (fig. 3–15): genus *Rhithrogena*
2b. Gills one and seven not modified as above . . . 3

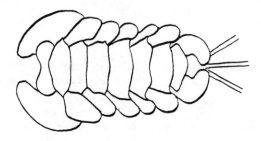

Fig. 3–15. Underside of abdomen of *Rhithrogena* mayfly nymph showing enlarged gills

3a. Gill seven filamentous, one to six oval, tails widespread and quite rigid: genus *Stenonema*
3b. Gill seven distinctly oval, although smaller than gill six . . . 4

4a. Head clearly notched at center of front edge (view from above as in fig. 3–16): genus *Cinygmula*
4b. Head without distinct notch at front . . . 5

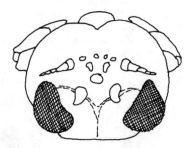

Fig. 3–16. Head of *Cinygmula* mayfly nymph. Note notch at center front of head.

5a. Oval gill on segment one less than one-half length of gill on segment two: genus *Cinygma*
5b. Oval gill on segment one only a tiny bit smaller than gill on segment two: genus *Heptagenia*

III Crawling and swimming nymphs

1a. Nymph with two tails; small insect three to six millimeters; antennae arising very low on head, appear to come from mouth (fig. 3–17): family Baetidae, genus *Pseudocloeon*

1b. Nymph with three tails . . . 2

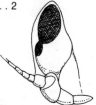

Fig. 3–17. Side view of head of *Pseudocloeon* mayfly nymph. Note position of antenna.

2a. Top of thorax greatly enlarged into prominent hump that extends back over first five segments of the abdomen (fig. 3–18): family Baetiscidae, genus *Baetisca*

2b. Top of thorax not enlarged . . . 3

Fig. 3–18. Humpbacked nymph of *Baetisca* mayfly

3a. Nymph with three tails of equal length . . . 4

3b. Nymph with three tails, center tail distinctly shorter than outer two tails; tails heavily fringed; slender head tilted downward; antennae arising about midway between eye and mouth; gill plates on abdominal segments one to seven; nymphs four to ten millimeters; (fig. 3–19): family Baetidae, genus *Baetis.* Note: in three western species the center tail is absent and the nymph may be confused with *Pseudocloeon,* check position of antennae.

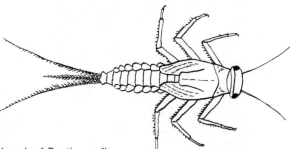

Fig. 3–19. Nymph of *Baetis* mayfly

4a. Small nymphs two to seven millimeters, average three to four; first gill enlarged to cover remaining gills . . . 5

4b. All gills visible, first gill not enlarged to cover other gills . . . 7

5a. First gill with triangular outline (fig. 3–20): family Tricorythidae, genus *Tricorythodes*

5b. First gill with nearly rectangular outline (fig. 3–21): family Caenidae . . . 6

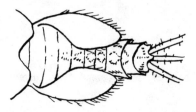

Fig. 3–20. Operculate gills of *Tricorythodes* mayfly nymph

Fig. 3–21. Operculate gill of Caenidae mayfly nymphs

6a. Head with three prominent hornlike projections (fig. 3–22): genus *Brachycerus*

6b. Head without prominent hornlike projections: genus *Caenis*

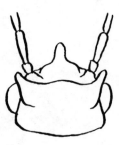

Fig. 3–22. Head of *Brachycerus* mayfly nymph. Note projections.

7a. Gills on abdominal segments three to seven or four to seven, oval, more wide than long; spines well developed at sides of abdomen (fig. 3–4): family Ephemerellidae, genus *Ephemerella*

7b. Gills occurring on abdominal segments one to seven . . . 8

8a. Gills single (in some species the first two gills may be double, but the rest are single) . . . 9

8b. All gills double, both parts may be similar in shape *or* one may be oval and the other bushy *or* one may be smaller than the other . . . 11

9a. Small nymphs, three to six millimeters long; gills oval: family Baetidae, genus *Cloeon*

9b. Nymph medium-sized, six to sixteen millimeters long; outer rear edge of each abdominal segment drawn out into a sharp, flattened spine (nymph has general appearance and shape of genus *Isonychia* (which see), but gills do not have basal tuft of feathery secondary gills and nymph lacks strong middorsal stripe) . . . 10

10a. Claw on front leg forked (with two points), other claws single; nymph with three longitudinal stripes on underside of abdomen: family Metretopodidae, genus *Siphloplecton*

10b. All claws single; gills one and two double, others all single, all gills oval: family Siphlonuridae, genus *Siphlonurus*

11a. Gills forked or deeply lobed: family Leptophlebiidae . . . 12

11b. Gills not forked, may be feathery or oval . . . 13

12a. All gills distinctly forked (fig. 3–23); nymphs six to eight millimeters long; head squarish: genus *Paraleptophlebia*

12b. Gills on first abdominal segment forked, all other gills lobed or scalloped like a maple leaf (fig. 3–24); ten to fourteen millimeters long: genus *Leptophlebia*

Fig. 3–23. Forked gill of *Paraleptophlebia* mayfly nymph

Fig. 3–24. Gill of *Leptophlebia* mayfly nymph

13a. Gills double and oval, secondary gill smaller (fig. 3–25); nymph often with dark band on tip (apical end) of tails: family Baetidae, genus *Callibaetis*
13b. Gills double, secondary gill tufted (fig. 3–26); tails heavily fringed; forelegs heavily fringed; body same width from head to tail; strong mid-dorsal stripe present (fig. 3–3): family Siphlonuridae, genus *Isonychia*

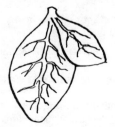   

Fig. 3–25. Double gill of *Callibaetis* mayfly nymph   Fig. 3–26. Double gill of *Isonychia* mayfly nymph

Adults

1a. Insect with three tails . . . I
1b. Insect with two tails . . . 2

2a. Tarsus of hind leg with four or fewer joints (fig. 3–27) . . . II
2b. Tarsus of hind leg with five moveable joints (fig. 3–28), four cubital intercallary veins (veins along inner rear edge) in fore wing (fig. 3–29) . . . III

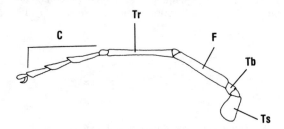

Fig. 3–27. Typical mayfly leg with four tarsal joints. C, coxa; Tr, trocanter; F, femur; Tb, tibia; Ts, tarsus

Fig. 3–28. Hind tarsus of Heptageniidae mayfly adult showing five movable joints

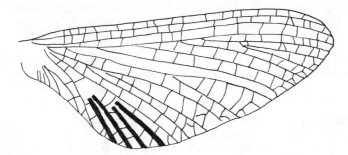

Fig. 3–29. Fore wing of Heptageniidae mayfly adult showing four intercallary veins

I Mayflies with three tails

1a. Insect with only one pair of wings (look closely with hand lens); very small (average three to six millimeters); eyes of both males and females very small; body brown, black, or creamy gray; dun with white wings; spinner with clear wings . . . 2

1b. Insect with two pairs of wings (hind pair may be quite small so look closely) . . . 4

2a. Cross veins present in front edge of wing (fig. 3–9): family Tricorythidae, genus *Tricorythodes;* Tricos

2b. Cross veins lacking in front edge of wing: family Caenidae . . . 3

3a. Plate on underside of thorax and between forelegs rectangular in shape and at least two times wider than long: genus *Brachycerus;* White Winged Red Brown

3b. Plate between forelegs triangular in shape and at least two times longer than wide: genus *Caenis;* Anglers Curse

4a. Two middle segments of abdomen much longer than other segments; top of thorax greatly enlarged; wings of dun often strongly mottled; outer two tails about four-fifths length of body, center tail very short; tarsus with five moveable joints: family Baetiscidae, genus *Baetisca;* Humpback Mayfly

4b. Two middle segments of abdomen similar in size to other segments; thorax not humpbacked . . . 5

5a. Insect nearly pure white, moderate sized (nine to twelve millimeters); wings with purple cast; thorax with tan cast; middle and hind legs of male and all legs of female feeble and nonfunctional; late summer hatch: family Polymitarcyidae, genus *Ephoron* (see also II, 1a); White Fly

5b. Insect colored (not white); all legs of both sexes functional . . . 6

6a. Dun wings yellowish or brownish; cross veins of wings very prominent due to dark coloration (easily seen with unaided eye) and/or wings heavily spotted . . . 7

6b. Dun wings gray (possibly with yellow front edge, but not spotted); cross veins no more noticeable than long veins; spinner wings clear; body usually shades of brown, yellow, or olive . . . 8

7a. Wings of dun with yellow cast; cross veins of wings of dun and spinner dark in color, long veins pale colored; body yellowish; moderate to large insects (eight to sixteen millimeters): family Potamanthidae, genus *Potamanthus;* Golden Drake

7b. Wings of dun brownish, wings of dun and spinner heavily spotted with brown, cross veins dark brown; body shades of yellow, green, or brown; large mayflies (eleven to twenty-five millimeters): family Ephemeridae, genus *Ephemera;* Green Drake (eastern), Brown Drake, Yellow Drake, and others

8a. Fore wing with short, detached veinlets along entire rear edge; hind wing with distinct bump near base of front edge (fig. 3–30): family Ephemerellidae, genus *Ephemerella;* Hendrickson, Sulphur, Blue Winged Olives, Red Quill, Pale Morning Dun, Green Drake (western), and others

8b. Fore wing without detached veinlets along rear edge; front edge of hind wing smooth, without strong projection: family Leptophlebiidae . . . 9

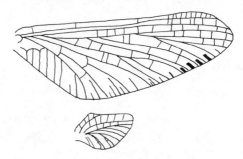

Fig. 3–30. Fore wing and hind wing of *Ephemerella* mayfly adult

9a. Generally small flies (average six to eight millimeters); wing veins not colored differently than cells; body rusty brown to mahogany brown; males may have white segments in center of abdomen: genus *Paraleptophlebia;* Blue Quill

9b. Generally medium-sized flies (average ten to thirteen millimeters); wing veins of dun and spinner dark brown; wings occasionally with large patches of rusty brown; body dark rusty brown: genus *Leptophlebia;* Black Quill

II Insect with two tails, hind tarsus with four or fewer joints

1a. Hind and middle legs of male and all legs of female feeble and nonfunctional; insect nearly pure white; moderate size (nine to twelve millimeters); cast husk of dun often remaining attached to tails; late summer hatch: family Polymitarcyidae, genus *Ephoron;* White Fly. Note: males and some females have two tails, most females have three tails (see also I, 5a).

1b. All legs of both sexes functional; insect not as described above . . . 2

2a. Insect with only one pair of wings (hind wings missing, look very closely with hand lens); eyes of male raised above surface of head into turban shape (fig. 3–31); insect small (three to six millimeters) . . . 3

2b. Insect with two pairs of wings (hind wings may be very small so look closely with hand lens) . . . 4

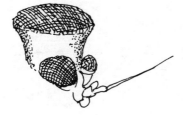

Fig. 3–31. Turbanate eye of Baetidae mayflies

3a. Veinlets along rear edge of wing detached and occurring in pairs (easiest to see in spinner, fig. 3–32): family Baetidae, genus *Pseudocloeon;* Tiny Gray-Winged Olive

3b. Veinlets along rear edge of wing occurring singly: family Baetidae, genus *Cloeon;* Tiny Gray-Winged Red Quill

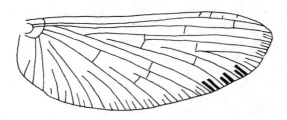

Fig. 3–32. Fore wing of *Pseudocloeon* mayfly adult

4a. Hind wing *very* small relative to fore wing (not easily seen with the unaided eye, check closely with hand lens); hind wing narrow, edges parallel . . . 5

4b. Hind wing visible with unaided eye, broadly triangular shape . . . 6

5a. Hind wing with thumb-shaped projection near base of front edge (fig. 3–33), three veins in hind wing; veinlets along rear edge of fore wing paired; eyes of male raised into turban shape; small to medium-sized mayflies (four to nineteen millimeters, average six millimeters); usually shades of olive or brown: family Baetidae, genus *Baetis;* Blue-Winged Olive. Note: if hind wing very small and filamentous with only two veins, then genus *Centroptilium;* Pale Watery Dun, Tiny Red Quill; rare in spring creeks.

5b. Hind wing with bump near base of front edge but bump not protracted into pointed thumb-shaped projection; wing veins (especially cross veins) white; wings with fancy spots and marks; bodies distinctly freckled with gray or brown; medium-sized insects (seven to twelve millimeters); common in lakes and slow streams: family Baetidae, genus *Callibaetis;* Speckled-Wing Dun

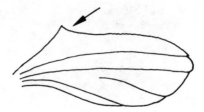

Fig. 3–33. Hind wing of *Baetis* adult showing pointed, thumb-shaped projection on basal foremargin

6a. Eyes of male insect touching on top of head . . . 7

6b. Eyes of male separated on top of head by distance about equal to width of one eye; wings with very prominent, dark colored long veins and cross veins; fore wing frequently with yellow along front edge; wing of spinner with colored margins; body yellow or with yellow markings; very large mayflies (fifteen to forty millimeters, most near larger end of scale — largest mayflies in North America): family Ephemeridae, genus *Hexagenia;* Giant Michigan Mayfly, Great Mahogany Drake, and others

7a. Wings of dun brown and mottled; wings of spinner marked with brown, veins brown; tarsus of front leg of male three times or more length of tibia; body usually brown; medium-sized insects (nine to thirteen millimeters); *strong* fliers; eastern and midwestern states: family Metretopodidae, genus *Siphlo-plecton;* Speckled Olive

7b. Wings of dun gray; spinner wings clear (margin may be colored but wings are not spotted); tarsus of front leg of male about equal in length to tibia . . . 8

8a. Abdomen of insect gray to purple gray and strongly barred with brown giving insect appearance of being ringed with alternate bands of gray and brown; wings of dun gray, those of spinner clear, not mottled; hind wing rather large and triangular in shape; eyes of male turban-shaped and distinctly barred (fig. 3–34); medium-sized insects (nine to twelve millimeters): family Siphlonuridae, genus *Siphlonurus;* Gray Drake

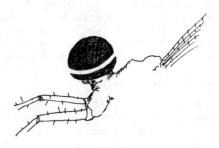

Fig. 3–34. Head of *Siphlonurus* mayfly adult showing barred eye

8b. Abdomen of insect rusty brown; dun wings slate gray, fore wing has clear area in its center; wings of spinner are clear with colored margins; forelegs rusty brown, hind two pairs of legs yellowish; medium large insects (nine to sixteen millimeters): family Siphlonuridae, genus *Isonychia;* White-Gloved Howdy, Leadwing Drake. Note: don't confuse these insects with the much larger but similar appearing *Hexigenia atrocaudata* which has very long, dark tails and a purple brown band entirely encircling the hind wing, see 6b above.

III Insect with two tails; hind tarsus with five moveable joints; four cubital intercallary veins (veins along inner rear edge) in fore wing: family Heptageniidae. Note: family Baetiscidae has five moveable joints in tarsus and center tail very short, it might at first glance appear as if these insects have only two tails, check I, 4a.

1a. Outer leading edge of fore wing with fine vein running parallel to front edge (fig. 3–35); western United States: genus *Cinygma*

1b. Fine vein lacking in outer leading edge of fore wing . . . 2

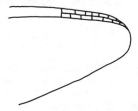

Fig. 3–35. Outer end of fore wing of *Cinygma* mayfly adult showing fine vein at outer front edge

2a. First segment of tarsus of front leg as long or longer than second segment; eyes of males touching on top of head; body color variable; wings of dun uniformly gray; spinner wings clear; cross veins at base of front edge of wing detached at front end (fig. 3–36); genus *Epeorus;* Quill Gordon (or Gordon Quill), Little Marryat, Blue Quill, and others

2b. First segment of tarsus of front leg of male shorter than second segment; distance between eyes variable . . . 3

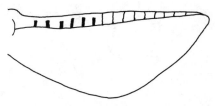

Fig. 3–36. Fore wing of *Epeorus* mayfly adult showing detached cross veins in basal front edge

3a. Cross veins in wings of dun prominently darkened giving wings a mottled appearance; eyes of males often fading to fluorescent colors of blue, green, or yellow in daylight; many species light colored (creams and tans) . . . 4

3b. Cross veins not strongly darkened; cross veins at tip of leading edge of wing branched (fig. 3–37); third section (femur) of foreleg with dark stripe running lengthwise down center; first segment of tarsus of front leg one-third or less the length of segment two: genus *Rhithrogena;* Red Quill

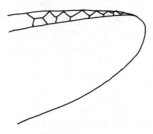

Fig. 3–37. Outer end of fore wing of *Rhithrogena* mayfly showing net of veins in outer front edge

4a. First segment of tarsus of front leg two-thirds or more as long as second segment; penes cleft to base (fig. 3–38); most species occur in western United States: genus *Cinygmula;* Western Gray Fox and others

4b. First segment of tarsus usually less than one-half length of second segment; penes fused and only cleft for a short distance . . . 5

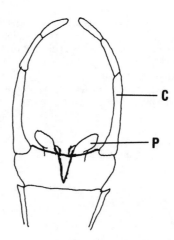

Fig. 3–38. Claspers and penes of *Cinygmula* mayfly adult male. C, clasper; P, pene

5a. Penes distinctly L-shaped, very angular (fig. 3–39): genus *Stenonema;* Gray Fox, American March Brown, Light Cahill, and others

5b. Penes not angular, may be curved, but not with strong L-shape: genus *Heptagenia;* Pale Evening Dun

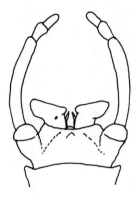

Fig. 3–39. Claspers and penes of *Stenonema* mayfly adult male

4

Stoneflies

NYMPHS

Stoneflies, like mayflies, are aquatic insects with an incomplete metamorphosis. At present, 465 species have been described for North America. They are in the order Plecoptera (*pleco,* folded; *ptera,* wing; referring to the folded hindwing of the resting adult).

The nymphs of stoneflies are found in well-oxygenated rivers and along the shorelines of lakes where wave action maintains a high oxygen level. They are called stoneflies because the nymphs are often found among stones in such places. This name is misleading, since any well-oxygenated waters may contain stoneflies, regardless of the bottom structure. Most species, in fact, prefer a specific habitat. A few prefer large boulders, some inhabit only coarse gravel and stony areas, others seek out fine gravels. Moss is chosen by several species while silty, slow flowing areas are sought by others. Many species congregate in areas where leaves and other debris accumulate. A few species are subterranean, living in water-saturated soils. Smaller species are herbivorous, but most larger nymphs are predatory and may rapaciously crop the immature forms of other insects. The nymphs tend to be drably colored and secretive, but trout seem especially fond of these insects and feed on them whenever encountered. A nymphal imitation fished along the bottom can be productive in waters harboring stoneflies.

Fig. 4–1. Bottom view of *Pteronarcys* stonefly nymph showing bushy gills at leg bases

When the egg masses are deposited, they break apart and the individual eggs sink and adhere tightly to bottom structures. Nymphs may hatch in a week or two or the eggs may remain dormant for months before hatching. Even eggs from the same female may hatch at different times. The young nymphs seek shelter, and as they grow, molt many times. Shedding of the skin seems to be a night activity, and the nymph is pale for several hours after changing skins.

The fully matured nymph varies in size from six to as many as seventy-five millimeters in length, depending upon species. In the smaller insects, gills are generally lacking. A few have simple, finger-shaped gills. The large stonefly nymphs in the families Pteronarcidae and Perlidae have clumped, bushy gills that are very obvious. Gills occur on the underside of the insect, usually near the bases of the legs (fig. 4–1). The three segments of the thorax are clearly visible, and both fore wing and hind wing pads are strongly developed (fig. 4–2). Stoneflies have only two tails. The absence of gills along the *abdomen* and the presence of *two* well-developed sets of wing pads distinguish stonefly nymphs from those of the mayflies.

At maturity, which is reached in one to four years, the nymphal skin splits

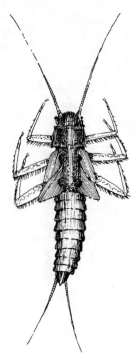

Fig. 4–2. Top view of *Pteronarcys* stonefly nymph. Note two pairs of wing pads and lack of abdominal gills.

along the top of the thorax and the adult emerges. A very few of the smaller species emerge at the surface of the water in the same manner as mayflies, and imitations should be fished accordingly. In most species, the nymphs crawl into the shallows seeking suitable emergence sites or leave the shelter of the rubble and drift in the currents, struggling ineptly to reach the streamside. Once there, they crawl onto the bank, boulders, logs, bridge abutments, and so forth, and undergo transformation to the adult (fig. 4–3). Large species often crawl high into trees before the adults emerge. During this migration to emergence sites, the nymphs are especially vulnerable to predation (fig. 4–4); an imitation fished near these places can be highly effective. Recently cast nymphal husks should alert the angler to the excellent fishing available when these insects are emerging.

Behavioral drift among stonefly nymphs seems to be confined to the smaller, herbivorous species. *Nemoura* nymphs are frequently reported in drift samples. *Alloperla, Isogenus,* and *Arcynopteryx* (family Perlodidae) nymphs also have been reported. The larger, predatory forms such as *Pteronarcys* and *Acroneuria* drift not at all or only rarely. They may, however, be part of the constant or catastrophic drift. Prior to a hatch, the

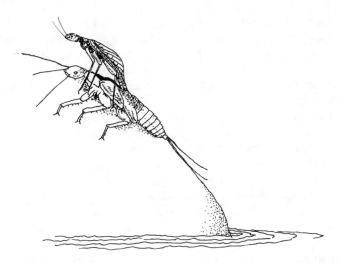

Fig. 4–3. Stonefly nymphs crawl from the water before the adult emerges.

Fig. 4–4. Trout feed heavily when stonefly nymphs are on the move.

emerging species drift in large numbers as the nymphs migrate to shore.

In many of the large western rivers, the big stoneflies are the dominant insects. In addition to their prodigious numbers, the nymphs of these species require two, three, or possibly four years to mature, hence are found year round. Trout capitalize on this abundant fare, and western fishermen should not be without an assortment of stonefly nymphs. The big nymphs should be fished deep and tumbled along the bottom like a dislodged natural. Often this technique requires weighted flies and sinking lines. The fly is cast quartering upstream to permit it time to sink. When the line reaches the point downstream where it begins to swing across the currents, the rod tip is lifted and the fly worked with a pulsing motion. After the line has swung across the stream, it is retrieved with a slow hand-twist until it can be easily pulled from the water. The fish may take the fly during any point of the drift. Most likely, however, the strike will come when the line reaches the quartering downstream point, for it is there that the fly lifts off the bottom and rises to the surface, triggering the predatory, chase instinct of the trout. Placing the line so that the fly arrives at a promising lie at this downstream point will increase the angler's success. When the cast is fished out, the angler moves one step downstream and repeats the process.

Heavy tackle is the order of the day when fishing these weighted, streamer-sized patterns. Leaders for such bottom probing must be short (fifty inches or less) to keep the fly on the bottom. They also must taper to not less than 2X (.009-inch diameter). Not only will lighter tippets fray and break from the weight of the fly as it's cast, but the lunging take of a large trout against a sinking line will severely tax all but the heaviest tippets.

The imitation I prefer for these big stonefly nymphs has a flat nylon or Swannundaze abdomen and a dubbed fur thorax. The shiny, well-segmented abdomen and fuzzy thorax of this pattern mimic the natural's features. Tying techniques are described in the appendix.

Smaller western stoneflies of importance are principally those of the genera *Capnia, Allocapnia, Taeniopteryx, Isoperla,* and *Alloperla.* Species of the first three genera hatch during warm afternoons in January through March and often into April. These winter hatching species are readily taken by the fish, and on open waters produce excellent midwinter angling — the perfect prescription for cabin fever. The adults are usually dark brown to black and about eight to twelve millimeters long. A fly of the correct coloration and size and tied like the Poly-Caddis is an excellent representation. Adults of *Alloperla* and *Isoperla* hatch during the midsummer months, usually during the late afternoon and evening; these insects are also well imitated by the Poly-Caddis pattern. These flies are eight to fifteen millimeters long and shades of green, chartreuse, yellow, and olive brown. Like the smaller winter stoneflies, these brightly colored insects usually mean good fishing.

Nymphs of these smaller stoneflies are readily accepted by the trout, often in preference to the adults. Watch for fish rolling in the shallows or flashing among the rocks. They are intercepting the nymphs as they migrate from protective cover to the emergence areas. During such feeding activity, the fly should be fished on a floating or intermediate line. The latter is a line that sinks very slowly. If greased with a fly floatant it will float; ungreased, it sinks. If a floating line is used, the leader butt can be greased, and when a fish takes the fly the greased portion of the leader will jerk under — a simple and effective strike indicator.

While the flat nylon technique works well for tying smaller nymphs, I prefer the Red Brown pattern for these flies. Tied in the red brown color, it is a fine imitation of many winter hatching species; in golden olive, lime green, and brownish olive it imitates the summer forms.

The eastern United States has not been blessed with the profuse hatches of big stoneflies that western anglers enjoy; nonetheless, stoneflies are important to the eastern fisherman. Many large nocturnal species of stoneflies are found in the East, including the Giant Black Stonefly *(Pteronarcys dorsata),* largest of the U. S. plecopterans.

Eastern anglers may be unfamiliar with the large stoneflies of their area since these species are all nocturnal. The big flies are principally of the families Pteronarcidae and Perlidae and hatch from April through July. The adults are occasionally seen in early morning as they emerge or in late evening as they return to oviposit. Big hair-wing imitations fished wet or dry are effective during the night and early morning hours when a hatch is in progress. However, the nymphs of these big insects are the most important forms for the eastern angler. Like their western counterparts, these nymphs require two to four years to mature, and the trout are well acquainted with them. The Giant Black Stonefly ranges in color from blackish brown to deep gray. *Paragnetina* (family Perlidae) are dark on the dorsal surface and pale beneath. *Acroneuria* (family Perlidae) are mottled ambers.

The streamer-sized imitations of these nymphs are fished like the western species. During June and early July when emergence is peaking, the predawn and very early morning period can be especially productive. Very large fish are often intercepted during this period. Emergence sites — boulders, logs, bridge abutments, and so forth — can be located by looking for the castoff nymphal skins. Work the artificial on a floating line.

Several small species of eastern stoneflies are diurnal and can produce good periods of daylight fly fishing; these include species of *Taeniopteryx, Alloperla,* and *Isoperla.* Some species of the winter hatching *Capnia* and *Allocapnia* are found in the East, but since most eastern states close the trout season during the colder months, these flies are only a curiosity to the fisherman. In those few eastern states where some waters are open to year-round angling, the winter species can provide good fishing. The Early Brown Stonefly *(Taeniopteryx fasciata)* emerges in heavy flights during March and April. In years with an early spring, these flights often end prior to the opening of trout season. In cooler years, the hatches are delayed and fine dry fly and nymph fishing can be had in the early weeks of the season. The adult is imitated well by either poly-wing or hair-wing patterns in rusty

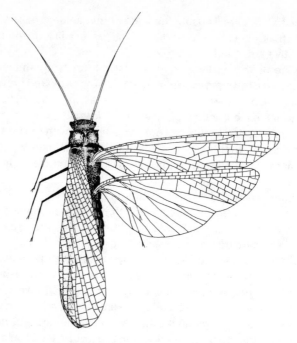

Fig. 4–5. An adult stonefly showing right wings extended and left wings folded in characteristic resting position

brown. The Red Brown Nymph is an excellent representation of the nymph. As with western species, those of the eastern *Alloperla* and *Isoperla* hatch at midseason. These yellow to green insects can produce fine fishing.

ADULTS

Stoneflies emerge during every month of the year; as many as one-third of the species of Plecoptera emerge, feed, and mate during the coldest months, a characteristic shared only with the midges. Once free from the nymphal fetters, the adults move away from the water, often for substantial distances, and seek a mate.

Adult stoneflies do not always have wings. The males of many species and the females of a few species are entirely wingless. Winged adults have two pairs of wings; the hind pair are much wider than the fore pair (fig. 4–5). At rest the wings are held along the top of the body. The hind wing is pleated and folded, giving this order of insects its name. The adults are clumsy fliers with the body often held vertical and the wings horizontal (at right angles to the position assumed by most insects during flight, fig. 4–6).

Fig. 4–6. Stonefly adults often fly with the body vertical and the wings horizontal.

In some species, the adults feed on algae or other vegetation; often food is required before the eggs can develop. In other species, the adults do not feed since they lack well-developed mouth parts, but do drink water. The adult lifespan is variable. Both sexes of species that do not feed and males of many species that do feed live for only a few days. Females that feed often live as long as four to five weeks.

Stoneflies do not form mating flights. Rather, in North American species, the males and females locate one another by drumming. The male taps his abdomen against the ground, branch, or whatever he's sitting on. Each species has a unique drumming pattern. If a female is nearby and feels the vibrations of the drumming, she replies. The male then moves toward the female and drums again. In this way they eventually meet and mate. The female will not mate again. Males may mate several times.

After mating takes place, the females return to the water to oviposit. Unlike mayflies and caddises, the females don't fly upstream before laying their eggs. However, their march away from and return to the water is generally upstream, which compensates for the downstream displacement of emerging nymphs. In some species, the nymphs migrate upstream before emergence.

Fall and winter hatching species usually deposit their eggs by alighting on the water's surface and releasing them or by crawling down into the water to place the eggs directly on the bottom. Spring and summer forms may simply drop the egg masses into the water while flying over it or may alight on the surface to release them.

Stonefly adults can produce good rises of fish. When emerging, they are frequently blown onto the water, but it is during periods of egg laying that they become of marked significance. Smaller species are sometimes overlooked by the angler, but good fish will feed when the flights are heavy. A Poly-Caddis of correct color is a fine imitation of the smaller species. Emergence of the big stones in early summer marks a period of excellent night fishing for the eastern angler. Where the flies are profuse, they will be active in the evening, after dark, and in the early morning.

The larger stoneflies produce some of the most important hatches on the turbulent rivers of the western United States. There, many species emerge and oviposit during the day. The Giant Salmon Fly *(Pteronarcys californica)* forms blizzard-like flights on the large western rivers of the Rocky and Sierra Nevada Mountains during June and July, and even the largest trout rise greedily to these salmon-pink flies. The Golden Stonefly or California Salmon Fly *(Acroneuria californica)* is another large stonefly of significance in the West, especially in the Pacific Northwest where it forms a major hatch on many rivers. This insect usually emerges with or just after the Giant Salmon Fly. The Willow Flies (other *Acroneuria* and species of family Perlidae) emerge during this same period and are often mixed with these other large stonefly hatches. Emergence starts in the lower reaches of a river and progresses upstream at a rate of several miles a day. Fishermen usually float the rivers during this time to cover more water and thus increase their chances of passing through the section of river where hatching and egg laying are in active progress. Wading can also be very productive.

Dry fly fishing during heavy flights can be very rewarding, but the fisherman may find the trout difficult simply due to an overabundance of natural food. In this case, a steadily rising trout should be selected and the fly presented again and again, timing the casts to correspond to the rise interval. The drift of the fly should be short (four to five feet) and the placement accurate. Often a twitch of the fly will raise a reluctant fish. Inconsistently feeding fish can be pounded up in the same manner, but usually require a more concentrated effort. During periods when fewer insects are on the water, cast to good holding lies and drift the fly as long as possible.

The rise to these flies is spectacular, and as with other large imitations, the angler should hesitate for a fraction of a second before tightening. This pause permits the trout to close his jaws on the fly, assuring a good hold for the hook.

Fig. 4–7. Bright memories await those who fish the stonefly hatches on western rivers.

Naturals that fall onto the water often drown and are taken by the trout. Bait fishermen take advantage of this fact, fishing the adults along the bottom most successfully. The big adult imitations can be fished on a sinking line, drifting them deep with an occasional twitch; microshot on the leader puts the flies down quickly. Trout do not take these large patterns timidly, so rig the terminal tackle accordingly.

Trout seem especially fond of the big stoneflies, experiencing pattern and color hangovers for a week or more following a major hatch; thus, this period is often excellent fishing even if none of these insects is on the water. In fact, some fishermen feel this is the most productive fishing and shun the hatch to fish this late period; certainly there is less competition from other anglers. The same imitations should be used — the color and shape are important. Cast to good holding lies and attain the longest drift possible.

Trout see these insects when they stray onto the water or alight on the surface to oviposit: wings folded along the back, legs outstretched, and body forming a meniscus in the surface film. Flies such as the Sofa Pillow or Bird's Stone are good producers during the stonefly hatches. The pattern I prefer is built on the basic design of Bird's Stone and is tied with an air trapping, fur chenille body; a hair wing; and hackles trimmed top and bottom to achieve the low silhouette of the natural.

Keys to Stoneflies

Nymphs

1a. Gills branched and filamentous, appearing as bushy clump on underside of entire thorax . . . 2

1b. Gills are not branched and bushy, *or* gills only on first segment of thorax, *or* gills absent . . . 3

2a. Gills on underside of entire thorax *and* on first two abdominal segments (fig. 4–8): family Pteronarcidae, two genera — *Pteronarcys,* eight species, *Pteronarcella,* two species; widespread and common to abundant; prefer gravels and stones as habitat but will congregate in leaf packs and debris in stony, fast water areas; largest stoneflies, includes Salmon Fly and Giant Black Stonefly; require two, three, possibly four years to mature; emerge spring to midsummer

2b. Gills only on thorax, occur on all three segments: family Perlidae, eight genera, thirty-six species; widespread and common to abundant; prefer gravels and stones as habitat; next largest stoneflies after those in family Pteronarcidae, up to forty millimeters long; many important species such as the Willow Flies and Amber Stoneflies of the genera *Acroneuria, Paragnetina, Perlesta* and others; mature in one to three years, emerge all summer

3a. Body looks like roach (fig. 4–9); plates on underside of thorax forming extensions that overlap the segment behind: family Peltoperlidae, one genus — *Peltoperla,* thirteen species; found in cold mountain streams of East and West; live in leaf litter; medium-sized (twelve to eighteen millimeters); mature in two years; emerge in summer

3b. Body not roachlike; plates on underside of thorax not overlapping . . . 4

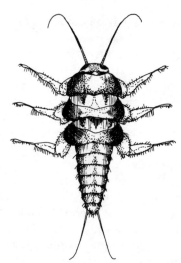

Fig. 4–8. Underside of *Pteronarcys* stonefly nymph showing gills on all three thoracic segments and the first two abdominal segments

Fig. 4–9. Top view of *Peltoperla* stonefly nymph

4a. Paraglossae and glossae of mouthparts about equal length (look at underside of head) (fig. 4–10) . . . 5

4b. Paraglossae extending well beyond glossae (fig. 4–11) . . . 8

Fig. 4–10. Paraglossae (P) and glossae (G) about equal in length

Fig. 4–11. Paraglossae (P) extending well beyond glossae (G)

5a. Second segment of tarsus as long or longer than first segment (fig. 4–12): family Taeniopterygidae, two genera; *Taeniopteryx,* nine species; *Brachyptera,* twenty-one species; widespread and common; occur in gravels and areas of accumulated debris and leaves; most noted for Early Brown Stonefly; one-year life cycle; emerge winter and spring

5b. Second segment of tarsus much shorter than first . . . 6

Fig. 4–12. Tarsus of Taeniopterygidae stonefly nymph

6a. Hind wing pads flared strongly outward from body; nymphs stout; hind legs reach well beyond tip of abdomen: family Nemouridae, one genus *Nemoura,* sixty-one species; widespread and common to abundant; inhabit gravels and debris; six to twenty millimeters long; one-year life cycle; emerge throughout the year

6b. Hind wing pads parallel body; nymphs elongated and slender; hind legs not reaching beyond end of abdomen . . . 7

7a. Top and bottom of abdominal segments one to nine separated by a membrane fold (fig. 4–13); abdomen flat on bottom, rounded on top when viewed in cross section (fig. 4–14): family Capniidae, six genera, 129 species, includes genera *Capnia, Isocapnia,* and *Allocapnia;* widespread and abundant; live in gravels and debris; four to nine millimeters long; one-year life cycle; emerge winter and early spring

7b. Membrane fold occurring at most on first six abdominal segments, that part of abdomen without membrane fold round in cross section: family Leuctridae, three genera, forty-five species; widespread and common; inhabit gravels and debris; six to eleven millimeters long; one- possibly two-year life cycle; emerge early spring through fall

Fig. 4–13. Abdomen of Capniidae stonefly nymph; side view showing membrane fold

Fig. 4–14. Cross sectional view of abdomen of Capniidae stonefly nymph; membrane fold occurs at bottom angles

8a. Body distinctly patterned, often bright yellow; tails same length, or longer than, abdomen; simple gills may be present: family Perlodidae, six genera, over ninety-seven species; includes genera *Isoperla* and *Isogenus;* widespread and common to abundant; prefer gravels; ten to twenty-five millimeters long; one-year life cycle; emerge spring through fall

8b. Body uniformly colored, many species yellow, chartreuse, or bright green; tails not more than three-quarters as long as abdomen; gills never present: family Chloroperlidae, six genera, fifty-nine species, includes genus *Alloperla;* widespread and common to abundant; prefer gravels; six to fifteen millimeters long; emerge spring through fall

Adults

1a. Paraglossae and glossae of mouth same length (fig. 4–10) . . . 2
1b. Paraglossae extending well beyond glossae (fig. 4–11) . . . 7

2a. Large insect, twenty-five to seventy-five millimeters long; body often shades of yellow or pink; gill remnants present on sides of first two abdominal segments; anal area of fore wing with two or more rows of cross veins (fig. 4–15): family Pteronarcidae

2b. Insects without gill remnants on abdomen; anal area of fore wing without cross veins (fig. 4–16) . . . 3

Fig. 4–15. Fore wing of Pteronarcidae stonefly adult showing two rows of anal crossveins

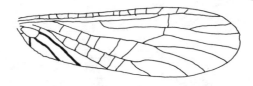

Fig. 4–16. Fore wing without anal crossveins

3a. Tails composed of five or six segments and much longer than width of first thoracic segment; insects four to nine millimeters long; dark colored: family Capniidae

3b. Tails no longer than width of first thoracic segment . . . 4

4a. Color dull brown; length six to eleven millimeters; tails one segmented; wings rolled around abdomen to give resting adult needle or stick appearance: family Leuctridae; Needleflies

4b. Wings not rolled around abdomen but held flat along top of body . . . 5

5a. Color straw to gray; ten to twenty-five millimeters long; two simple eyes on top of head; remains of gills on sides of at least middle and hind thoracic segments just above leg bases; top of first thoracic segment tipped down and forward (viewed from side): family Peltoperlidae

5b. Gill remnants lacking on thorax above leg bases; top of first thoracic segment in the same plane as tops of middle and hind segments . . . 6

6a. Second segment of tarsus same length as first, all three segments of tarsus of about equal length (fig. 4–12); brown to grayish in color: family Taeniopterygidae

6b. Second segment of tarsus much shorter than first segment. Tails one-segmented, dull colored grays and browns, six to twenty millimeters long: family Nemouridae

7a. Remnants of branched gills at lower angles of thoracic segments; ten to twenty-five millimeters long; body often shades of yellow at least on underside; tails much longer than width of thorax: family Perlidae

7b. Gill remnants lacking from thorax (note, in a *few* species there may be finger-shaped remnants of simple gills but *not* remnants of branched gills); colors often bright yellows and greens; tails longer than width of thorax . . . 8

8a. Forks of second anal veins of fore wing arising from anal cell (anal area of wing is located near its inner rear edge); hind wing with more than four anal veins (fig. 4–17): family Perlodidae

8b. Second anal vein of fore wing not forked or forked well beyond anal cell (fig. 4–18): family Chloroperlidae (note, western genus *Kathroperla* with anal veins like Perlodidae but recognizable because head decidedly longer than wide)

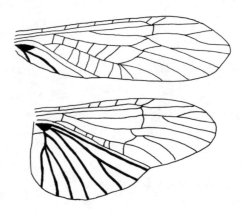

Fig. 4–17. Fore wing and hind wing of Perlodidae stonefly adult. Anal cell is solid black area near base of wing.

Fig. 4–18. Basal area of fore wing of Chloroperlidae stonefly adult. Note anal vein forked well beyond anal cell.

5

Caddisflies

The caddisflies are closely related to moths and butterflies; indeed, at one time entomologists placed them all in one order. The name "Trichoptera" of the order refers to the hairy covering on the wings (*tricho*, hair; *ptera*, wing). There are over nine hundred species of caddises in the United States and Canada, ranging in size from about three millimeters for some microcaddises to as much as forty millimeters for the Great Orange Sedge. They are widely distributed in our lakes and streams, and are second in abundance only to the Diptera. Thus, even in waters rich in other invertebrates, caddises are of major importance as trout food.

Herbert Ross, in his book *The Caddis Flies or Trichoptera of Illinois*, states that caddises are the most abundant insect in Midwest streams. The net-spinning caddises (family Hydropsychidae) far outnumber other Midwest species. Many eastern rivers have excellent caddis populations also, as anyone who has seen the profuse hatches of the American Grannom and White Miller will agree. Rivers of the western United States have been particularly blessed with caddises. The Firehole, Madison, Yellowstone, Henry's Fork, and many, many others have caddis hatches during the entire summer; often several species are on the water at the same time. Such nationwide profusion makes a thorough understanding of the Trichoptera essential.

Some anglers have suggested that the caddis population has grown in recent years because they can tolerate pollution better than mayflies. This is an oversimplification. Many caddisfly species require cold, clean water (hence the large number of species in the West). In fact, caddises originated in cold waters and representatives of all families are found there. Many mayflies are also intolerant of pollution. On the other hand, there are species of both caddises and mayflies that can tolerate both organic and thermal pollution. As streams become warm and loaded with wastes, the unfit species die. Those species that tolerate the changes live and increase dramatically as they fill the vacated spaces. Thus, as the total number of species decreases, the number of individuals in any remaining species increases, and they become more apparent to the observer.

Bill Hilsenhoff in the department of entomology, University of Wisconsin, Madison, has developed an accurate method of evaluating water quality through this differential tolerance to pollution. For example, he found the American Grannom *(Brachycentrus americanus)* and many others to be very intolerant to pollution while most microcaddises were very tolerant. He lists numerous species of aquatic insects and crustaceans and their relative tolerances in a paper entitled "Use of Arthropods to Evaluate Water Quality of Streams."

LARVAE

Trichoptera have complete metamorphosis: egg to larva to pupa to adult, this cycle usually requiring one year. Recent investigations have shown that some species have two broods per year and others may have a two-year life cycle. Some seem to have several generations each summer. Work in this area is far from complete.

The soft-bodied larva looks like a worm. It has six jointed legs but lacks wing pads. Many species construct cases around themselves, using stones, sand grains, or bits of vegetation, binding these building materials with silk secreted from special glands in the mouth. Because of these houses, caddis larvae are probably the most widely recognized of the immature aquatic insects. By undulating its abdomen, the larva can pull water through the case to increase its oxygen supply.

Crawling slowly along the bottom and dragging their cumbersome shelters, these omnivorous larvae capture other immature insects or ingest algae and diatoms with ease. Trout are one of their predators, scraping off the larvae and ingesting them case and all. Powerful digestive juices break down the body of the insect and the silk chinking of its case, leaving the gravel and bits of vegetation often found during stomach autopsies.

Many of the various families, genera, and even species of case-building larvae produce unique structures. Through careful observation, cases become as definitive as fingerprints. The American Grannom builds a slender, tapered case shaped like a square chimney and constructed of bits of vegetable detritus. The case of the White Miller *(Nectopsyche* spp.) resembles a tiny cornucopia made of sand grains, while members of the genus *Helicopsyche* build small shelters shaped like snail shells.

Cased caddis larvae may be more available to the trout than once thought. Of all the aquatic insects, the case-building caddises would seem the least likely to participate in behavioral drift, but in fact they do, and sometimes in a big way. As opposed to most insects, which drift at night, caddises are daytime drifters. The nationwide American Grannom and the western *Oligophlebodes sigma* are two species commonly cited in articles on drift. Both drift in their cases. I've observed the Grannom letting itself out on a silk thread and hanging in midwaters (fig. 5–1); this may well be part of drift behavior. *Glossosoma* larvae will leave their cases and drift. As more

Fig. 5–1. A *Brachycentrus* caddis larva letting itself out on a silk thread

work is done in this relatively new area, I feel confident more species will be added to the list of drifting caddises. Fly patterns to imitate these cased, free floating larvae should suggest the case with the insect poking part way out. Polly Rosborough's Blonde Burlap has proved excellent in this regard. In blonde and in a natural burlap color it suggests caddises with a sand or pebble case; in dark brown it matches the Grannom and others. Cased larvae of *Leptocerus americanus* and species of *Triaenodes* (both in the family Leptoceridae) are powerful swimmers. Their long hind legs are heavily fringed with hairs and act as paddles (fig. 5–2). These larvae are very active in the upper layers of plant beds in streams and lakes. *L. americanus* has a silk case; the *Triaenodes* species build a spiral case of plant fragments. A Blonde Burlap and an Olive Burlap are good imitations, respectively.

The net-spinning caddises build a permanent house and construct a net of sheerest silk nearby (fig. 5–3). They emerge from time to time to crawl over the net, feeding on microscopic organisms swept by the currents into the delicate snares. These larvae are highly uniform in appearance and have

Fig. 5–2. A *Leptocerus* caddis larva swimming in its case

Fig. 5–3. A Hydropsychidae caddis larva with its net

Fig. 5–4. Finger nets

large clusters of branched, filamentous gills on the underside of the abdomen. Other caddises spin finger-shaped or trumpet-shaped nets in which
they live and feed (fig. 5–4).

Some caddis larvae shun the habits of their order, preferring to live
entirely free. These free spirits include the brilliant Green Rock Worm
(*Rhyacophila* spp.) often found in the guts of early season trout. These
emerald beauties roam freely, searching out their prey, and in turn become
prey along with their more conservative, armored relatives. Most microcaddises are free living in youth but adopt pebble or silk lodgings as they
mature.

The free-living and net-spinning larvae are favorites with the fly tier. Dyed
monofilament imitates the accentuated segmentation of the natural's abdomen. Gills of ostrich herl can be added. The finished fly should extend
onto the bend of the hook, imitating the slight curve assumed by a dislodged, drifting natural. Ral Boaze, Jr. of Brunswick, Maryland, ties his
larval imitations with a latex abdomen. This style has received much attention in recent years and has proved very successful. Many anglers prefer a
dubbed fur or yarn abdomen for the caddis larvae. If these materials are
used, gills may be simulated by picking out the underside of the abdomen
with a bodkin or scissors point. Legs for the larvae imitations may be formed
from hair or hackle.

Larval patterns are best fished dead drift on a four- to six-foot-long tippet,
letting the fly follow the tongues of current among the bottom structures. A
tiny, fluorescent cork strike indicator is most helpful.

PUPAE

When the caddis larva reaches maturity (from six months to a year), it

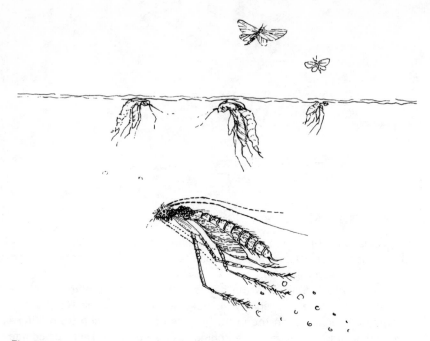

Fig. 5–5. A typical caddis pupa (pharate adult)

enters the pupal stage. Case-building caddisflies seal the case and cement it to the bottom. Free-living larvae construct a silken cocoon or sand grain pupation chamber. Inside, the insect undergoes a wonderful change. It actually becomes two insects in one. A pupal body develops, and as it matures, an adult forms inside. The pupal husk gives strong evidence of the internally developing adult. Wing pads form, curving down along the sides of the thorax, the antennae elongate enormously, the abdomen shortens, sucking mouthparts develop in the adult while the pupa retains powerful mandibles, and legs grow three times longer. Pupal legs are oarlike for swimming while adult legs are slender for running. When metamorphosis is complete, this strange adult in pupal dress is called a pharate adult (fig. 5–5).

Some groups are strictly spring emergers, others hatch in the fall, many emerge in the summer. Several emerge spring and fall, and some species such as *Helicopsyche boralis* apparently have a continuous succession of generations, for they emerge all summer long. Many emerge at night and consequently go unnoticed by the angler. The hatches may be concentrated with many individuals emerging at one time, or they may be sporadic and strung out all day. Hatching characteristics are nicely detailed in Eric

Leiser and Larry Solomon's book *The Caddis and the Angler.* Anyone who is seriously interested in these insects should read this text. It is the first angling work aimed exclusively at the caddises.

Using its specially reinforced mandibles, the pharate adult cuts out of the chamber. A number of species migrate along the bottom and climb out on shore or on other objects before the adult emerges. In some instances the pharate adult comes to the surface and swims on top as it heads to shore. Ray Ovington reports this phenomenon for the Green Rock Worm in his book *How to Take Trout on Wet Flies and Nymphs.* Other anglers have reported this peculiar activity for other species.

Many caddis adults emerge at the film. Once free of the pupation chamber, the insect pumps gasses between the pupal husk and the adult inside and pops to the surface like a cork. In his book *Challenges of the Trout,* Gary La Fontaine says that the pharate adult generates these gasses after cutting out of the chamber. Thus, the insect drifts along the bottom for a short ways before suddenly shooting for the surface, the adult operating the legs of the encasing pupal husk. Despite this ungainly arrangement, the pupa swims smoothly as it dashes from the protective cover of the bottom rubble to the film.

As the organism ascends, the external water pressure lessens and the pupal husk expands and bursts. This usually occurs in the surface film and the adult literally flies out of the water. Many species, however, must halt, at least momentarily, at the surface. In the film the husk ruptures at the back and the adult crawls forth — first wings, then head, then body and legs — pulling itself free from the fetters of aquatic existence. Eager for flight, the newly born insect tries its tender wings, fluttering momentarily on the surface. It may gain flight rather rapidly, or as happens with some of the larger caddises, it may buzz around on the surface for some time. This is the most vulnerable time in the caddis's life, and the trout devour them in great quantities, rolling and splashing in the pursuit. Confronted with such frenzied behavior on the part of the normally retiring trout, the fisherman often fails to recognize the feeding pattern (frequently confusing it with midge activity) and fruitlessly plies the water with a dry fly. During such times a good pupal imitation will provide some of the most exciting angling that can be experienced. The trout can literally tear the fly from the leader in its haste to capture the escaping imitation.

The pharate adult presents a unique silhouette. The pupal husk hangs on the adult like a revealing negligee and the gasses glow peculiarly. In *How to Take Trout on Wet Flies and Nymphs,* Ray Ovington writes about this curious caddis characteristic and describes dressings to simulate the pharate adult. He credits his friend Ed Sens with working out the details of emergence and developing the artificials. The flies had a floss abdomen on which fur was lightly spun and then picked out to imitate the pupal shuck. Working on this same theme, Gary La Fontaine created a fly with a dubbed body loosely covered by sparkle yarn. The sparkle yarn has proved to simulate well the glowing, double-walled insect.

The pupal imitations I like are lightly weighted and tied with soft bird hackle in the manner of the spider-type wet flies favored by Jim Leisenring and described in *The Art of Tying the Wet Fly and Fishing the Flymph.* His patterns were copies or variations of British flies such as the Snipe and Yellow, Grouse and Orange, Grouse and Green, and Woodcock and Yellow. These pattern names indicate the origins of the soft hackle used and the body color. Feathers from many birds are useful in pupal imitations: woodcock, snipe, grouse, pheasant, starling, jackdaw, crow, coot, mallard, and teal. The best feathers are usually those from the neck cape or the wing coverts. Bodies are of blended sparkle yarn, coarsely dubbed and well picked out, a wedding of the successful concepts of Sens and La Fontaine.

The "Leisenring lift" developed by, and named in honor of, the father of wet fly fishing in America is probably the best method ever devised for simulating the movements of emerging caddis pupae. Place the fly up and across stream, far enough above the holding lie of the trout so that the fly reaches the fish at its level. Follow the line with the rod and allow as little slack as necessary to keep the fly down. As the artificial approaches the holding position, check the rod and allow the currents to lift the fly to the surface. This technique requires some practice, but once mastered is deadly.

Fish will frequently feed on emerging adults. The pattern should float in the film and have a humpbacked silhouette. During July and August there are excellent hatches of huge, mottled gray *Limnephilus* caddises on western lakes. A yellowish green-bellied humpy tied with brownish olive deer hair was working well for me, but as I fished, an old eastern bass pattern, the Devil Bug, came to mind. This fly is essentially just a humpy body. Modified slightly it proved more effective than any other fly I tried for imitating the partially emerged adult. In lakes it may be simply cast out and allowed to sit motionless on the surface until intercepted by a cruising fish. Sometimes the newly emerged adults swim rapidly along the surface trying to get airborne, and an intentionally dragged Devil Bug elicits dramatic rises.

ADULTS

The most prominent feature of the adult caddisfly is its two pairs of wings, which are the same size, opaque, and one and one-half to two times the body length. At rest the wings are held over the back, parallel to the body and forming an inverted V, like a tent or roof (fig. 5–6). In flight, the caddis

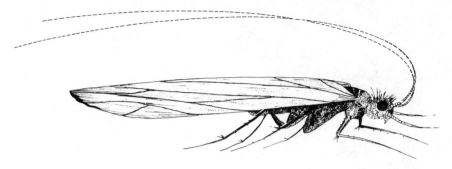

Fig. 5–6. A typical adult caddis

may be confused with a moth, but the identity of the resting adult is plain. These insects are usually drab and have very long antennae. They are equipped with limited sucking mouthparts adapted for ingestion of liquid foods; in spite of this, adults may live for two or more months, a one-month life span being the average.

During the day, caddisflies hide in dark crevices or on foliage near the water's edge and are often found clinging to the damp undersides of bridges — an excellent collecting site. In the evening, the insects become active and fly in great swarms over the surface of the water. Possibly because of very cold nights, autumn-hatching species are most active in the day.

Large flights during periods when there is no hatch probably represent the nuptial dance of the caddis. Mating takes place over land, and the females return to the water and deposit their eggs. Ovipositing may be accomplished by the female dipping down and touching the water to re-lease her egg mass, or eggs may be laid on vegetation just above the waterline, or the insect may crawl down into the water to deposit her eggs directly on the bottom structures. Trout feed on the adults that hatch in the film and on the females as they oviposit either on or below the surface.

Fortunately, the colors of caddises vary remarkably little. My adult caddis imitations include only seven basic color schemes, which form a most efficient working collection; these artificials are given in the appendix. Pharate adults are colored similarly to the adults.

The Poly-Caddis has become my favorite adult caddis pattern. It is useful not only when the naturals appear on the water surface in numbers, but also as an attractor pattern for periods of little apparent insect activity. The widespread presence of caddises in river systems of the United States and the sporadic hatching characteristics of many species constantly expose the trout to adult trichopterans. This accounts for the Poly-Caddis's suc-cess during non-hatch periods.

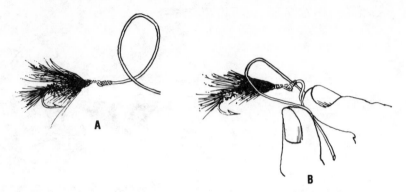

Fig. 5–7. The riffle hitch. Form a loop in the leader (A) and slip it over the head of the fly (B), drawing it tight just behind the head.

There are several methods for fishing adult caddisflies. In his book *Fishing the Dry Fly as a Living Insect,* Leonard Wright states that his pattern should be twitched slightly, immediately after landing on the water, then drifted free float for maximum effectiveness. This is an excellent technique. My experiences with the Poly-Caddis have produced some equally deadly tactics. Cast the fly directly downstream in broken, riffly water, and holding the rod high, *skip* (don't drag) the fly upstream. Drop the rod tip and allow the fly to run down the same lane of water where it was skipped. Repeat several times. Often this will provoke a strike. Another method that frequently produces savage strikes employs a riffle hitch (fig. 5–7). The hitched fly is fished in the riffles or the tail of a pool and simply allowed to drag down and back across the currents. Be ready! During a hatch or when females are ovipositing on the surface, it's best to dead drift the fly over a feeding fish since a dragging fly will often put such a fish down. However, if the dead drift does not produce results, try to hit the fish on the head, laying the fly directly on the rise as soon as possible. Be prepared for an instant response. All in all, the best advice might be to experiment. Watch the activity of the naturals and try to duplicate it with your fly.

Since the female often crawls under the surface to deposit her eggs, a wet fly fished during periods of ovipositing can be killing. As she enters the water, an air bubble forms around her abdomen, trapped there by wing and body hairs and transforming the drab Cinderella into a silver gowned princess. The Poly-Caddis has proved to be an excellent fly for mimicking subsurface adults; the poly yarn traps air and shimmers and glows like a living insect. Fish the fly without dressing it with floatant and twitch it on the retrieve.

In addition to crawling below the surface, gravid females may actually dive bomb into the water and swim rapidly to the bottom to deposit their ova. This unique habit was first described by Sid Gordon *(How to Fish from Top to Bottom)* for caddises he observed in June 1937, near Winneboujou Bridge on Wisconsin's Bois Brule River.

> As it pierced the water film, an almost unbelievable change came over that drab fly. It suddenly seemed to be encased in a bright gleaming bubble, so bright that it looked a shining ball of quicksilver. Fast moving legs propelled the bubble, angling it down toward the bottom . . . . Its fast moving legs, working like pistons, wholly outside the bright bubble, propel the fly swiftly like a swimming minnow. You will plainly see the body of the fly inside the bright envelope, and you will note that its wings do not move. It is the rough body and wings that create and hold the bubble by trapping air.

A Poly-Caddis can be used to mimic these insects quite effectively. Because of the rapid swimming motion of such insects, the artificial is worked with a jerky, stop-start retrieve. A microshot pinched on just ahead of the fly will cause it to dive and dart, aiding in the attempt to ape the swimming natural. The fish's take is always positive.

MICROCADDISES

Ernie Schwiebert has called the Firehole the "strangest trout stream on earth." It meanders through the major geyser basins of Yellowstone Park, passing by the steaming, hissing land and collecting the outfall from boiling bits of sulphurous water. But instead of having adverse effects, the water moderates the river's icy chill and adds carbonates, the essential ingredient of a highly productive stream. Rich beds of aquatic weeds and algae harvest the sun, storing the energy in their cells. Herbivores feed on these producers and in turn support the trout, the only fish in the upper river.

The large herbivores are chiefly insects, and while there are several species of mayflies, the Firehole is principally a river of caddises. Especially abundant are the microcaddises.

Brown and rainbow trout of the Firehole are fully aware of the rhythms of the microcaddis life cycle, for the insects are ubiquitous and legion in this watershed. Larvae, pupae, and adults are basic items in their diet, producing some of the most selective rises of any insect. Having experienced thousands of tourist hours of exposure to man and his lures, the fish feed serenely on the smallest of fare, disregarding larger, more easily imitated insects.

In the stretch along Fountain Freight Road, near the confluence of the Firehole and the smaller Nez Perce, the microcaddises produce almost

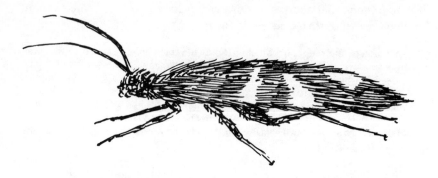

Fig. 5–8. A typical microcaddis adult

daily rises of ultrasophisticated fish. Fishing is dreamy: slow, gentle, and delicate. Tiny flies dressed on light wire hooks from #18 to #28 and held to the leader with .004- or .003-inch diameter tippets must be carefully presented and ever so carefully pulled home. The fish are strong and use the current advantageously, but with delicate pressure they are brought to net and held gently until they swim away.

Microcaddises certainly are not confined to the Firehole. These Hydroptilidae (and a few minute members of other families) occur across the United States in many types of waters. All are small (two to six millimeters long), very hairy, and usually black or mottled dark browns, although a few are tan (fig. 5–8). Anglers often suppose that fish rising to these insects are taking midges. Don't be fooled; check the film with a surface screen to confirm the insect group. During the hatch, trout will roll for pupae and dimple for the adults, sometimes taking both forms, sometimes concentrating exclusively on one or the other. The angler must pay close attention to the rise forms of the fish.

Microcaddis imitations must be realistic in their suggestion of color, form, size, and life. Larval imitations are so small that presenting them in a deep, free drift is nearly impossible, but they can be effective when fished under the film at the edges of weed beds. A dubbed fur body and throat of bird fibers is a most adequate imitation. A soft hackle fly replicates the flowing legs, robust thorax, and shiny body of the pupa. The abdomen is floss, the thorax is dubbed fur, and the legs are grouse or similar soft hackle. For the adults I use the Micro-Poly-Caddis.

Keys to Caddisflies

As a group, caddises are probably the second most difficult for the nonbiologist to classify (Diptera being first). The different caddises are amazingly uniform in many respects, and the number of species is very numerous. To separate them often requires the detailed examination of rather obscure body parts. Some larvae cannot be separated into species even by entomologists who have spent a lifetime studying caddises. The guide given below, however, is a good place to start a quest to understand more about these insects. Read through it, look at the drawings, and key out some larvae. After becoming somewhat familiar with the caddises, use the texts by Merritt and Cummins (1978), Wiggins (1977), and Ross (1944) for detailed study. Notes on the adults are also included below.

Overall length as given below is in millimeters for mature larvae and for adults. Adult length is overall, from head to end of wings. Color of an adult refers to the wings since these are its most prominent features.

Larvae

1a. Larva without case . . . 2
1b. Larva with case . . . 4

2a. Conspicuous, bushy gills on underside of abdomen (fig. 5–9); top of each thoracic segment covered with a single, large, hard plate; anal legs prominent (fig. 5–10): family Hydropsychidae, net spinning caddises, eleven genera, 142 species. Prevalent in fast water across United States. Larvae build net and permanent retreat (fig. 5–3); colors are gray to green; length thirteen to eighteen millimeters; pupate in retreat; emergence is rapid at the film. Adults emerge all summer; seven to eighteen millimeters long; cinnamon, mottled browns, mottled white and black, mottled cream and brown; antennae same length as body or slightly longer; females crawl underwater to lay eggs.

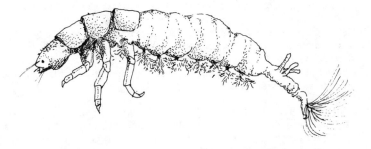

Fig. 5–9. Larva of Hydropsychidae caddis. Note abdominal gills.

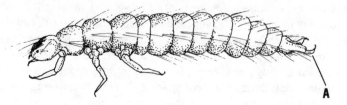

Fig. 5–10. Larva of *Rhyacophila* caddis. Note anal legs (A).

2b. Gills lacking; top of middle and last thoracic segment without plates or with several small plates . . . 3

3a. Ninth abdominal segment with hard plate on upper surface; anal legs prominent (fig. 5–10): family Rhyacophilidae, three genera, at least 104 species, over 100 in genus *Rhyacophila,* rock worms. Free living; larva often bright green (Green Rock Worm), ten to twenty millimeters in length; build gravel case for pupation; emergence is rapid at the surface, principally in spring. Adults eleven to thirteen millimeters long with dark blue-gray wings and green body; antennae shorter than body; females crawl or dive-bomb into water to lay eggs on bottom.

3b. Hard plate absent from ninth abdominal segment; anal legs prominent: three families: (1) Family Philopotamidae, finger net caddises, three genera, thirty-one species. Widespread in running waters; larva ten to twelve millimeters long, dirty white; build long, finger-shaped nets along underside of rocks in fast water; build domed, pebble pupation chamber on underside of rocks; emerge rapidly in film. Adults six to eight millimeters; black to brown; antennae shorter than body; females crawl under water to oviposit; includes chimarra caddis, one of earliest spring emergers. (2) Family Psychomyiidae, trumpet net caddises, five genera, fifteen species. Swift streams to ponds and lakes; larvae six to sixteen millimeters long; dirty white often marked with purple; spin funnel-shaped net that resembles a trumpet; a few species burrow in bottom and line this den with a silk sheath; emerge rapidly at surface. Adult four to twelve millimeters (most are on the short end of this range); reddish brown mottled browns, or straw colored; antennae shorter than body; crawl underwater to lay eggs. (3) Family Polycentropodidae, tube net caddises, seven genera, seventy-eight species. Swift streams to lakes and ponds; larvae four to fifteen millimeters long; pale gray to straw colored; most spin tube net which is open at both ends, some spin funnel-shaped net; rapid emergence in film. Adults six to eleven millimeters, browns and gingers; antennae shorter than body; crawl beneath water to lay eggs.

4a. Abdomen of larva significantly wider and/or deeper than thorax (fig. 5–11); larva very small (average three millimeters); case variable, silken sack to purse shape (figs. 5–11 and 5–12), case much larger than larva: family Hydroptilidae, microcaddises, thirteen genera, 170 species. Widespread in all waters; larvae free living in first four instars but build cases in last instar; emerge in film. Adults are three to five millimeters; very hairy; usually dark brown or mottled black and white; antennae shorter than body; crawl under water to lay eggs.

4b. Abdomen of larva similar in size to thorax; case fits snugly on larva . . . 5

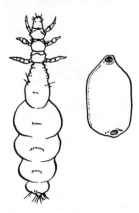

Fig. 5–11. Microcaddis *(Leucotrichia pictipes)* with silk case that it cements to stones. Case is much larger than larva. Note swollen abdomen of larva.

Fig. 5–12. Microcaddis in purse case of sand grains

5a. Case snail-shaped and composed of sand grains (fig. 5–13): family Helico-psychidae, one genus, *Helicopsyche,* four species. Abundant and widespread in streams and lakes; larvae about eight millimeters long, tan to brownish; emerge over the warm seasons. Adults five to seven millimeters; grayish brown to mottled browns; antennae shorter than body; oviposit in film or in wet areas next to stream or lake.

5b. Case linear or oval but not snail-shaped . . . 6

Fig. 5–13. Snail-shaped case of *Helicopsyche* caddis larva

6a. Case shaped like turtle shell (oval) and composed of sand grains (fig. 5–14); ninth segment of abdomen with hard plate on upper surface: family Glossosomatidae, six genera, seventy-nine species. Widely distributed in streams; larvae three to nine millimeters long; pinkish tan; emerge principally in spring, rapidly in film. Adults three to ten millimeters; dark brown; females crawl below surface to lay eggs.

6b. Case tube-shaped . . . 7

Fig. 5–14. Bottom view of turtle-shaped case of Glossosomatidae caddis larva

7a. Case of sand grains with distinct flanges at sides and hooded in front (fig. 5–15); claws of hind legs small; those of other legs large: family Molannidae, two genera, *Molanna,* widespread, six species and *Molannodes,* Alaska, one species (Note: if larva has prominent antenna and legs not as above, genus *Ceraclea,* family Leptoceridae). In gravel in lakes and slow water areas of rivers; larvae average fifteen to twenty millimeters long; straw colored; emerge in spring. Adults ten to sixteen millimeters long; mottled grays and browns; antennae same length as body; oviposit by crawling under water.

7b. Case without prominent hood and flanges, composed of sand, pebbles, or vegetable matter . . . 8

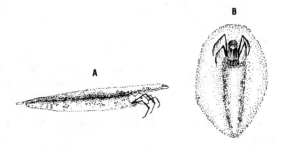

Fig. 5–15. Side view (A) and bottom view (B) of flanged case of Molannidae caddis larva

8a. Larva lacking spacing humps (fig. 5–16) on *both* top and sides of first abdominal segment: family Brachycentridae, six genera, thirty-one species; genus *Brachycentrus* is well-known American Grannom. Larvae build chimney cases that are square in cross section, tapered, and made of quite narrow plant fragments (fig. 5–17), other genera build similar cases of plant material or tapered cases of sand grains; larvae of family are six to twelve millimeters long, tan to bright green; emerge in spring, rapidly at surface. Adults six to eleven millimeters; dark brown to tawny wings; female with characteristic, bright green egg sack; antennae shorter than body; dip abdomen into water to oviposit.

8b. Spacing humps present, at least on sides of abdomen . . . 9

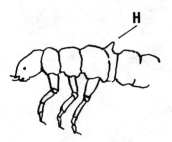

Fig. 5–16. Dorsal spacing hump on Limnephilidae caddis larva. H, hump

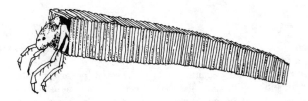

Fig. 5–17. *Brachycentrus* larva in its chimney-shaped case

9a. Spacing hump *lacking* from *top* of first abdominal segment, present on sides; antenna next to eye (look very closely with hand lens); case usually four-sided and made of plant fragments roughly square in shape (fig. 5–18), some have spiral cases, sand grain cases, or log cabin type cases (fig. 5–19): family Lepidostomatidae, two genera, seventy species; widespread in small cold streams in slower waters of large rivers and along lake edges; larvae six and one-half to nine millimeters long, cream to brownish. Adults eight to ten millimeters; mottled browns to grays; antennae shorter than body; oviposit at surface or in damp areas near stream.

9b. Spacing humps present on top and both sides of first abdominal segment . . . 10

Fig. 5–18. Case of Lepidostomatidae caddis larva

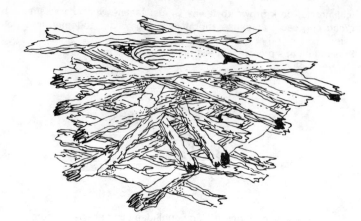

Fig. 5–19. Log cabin case of Limnephilidae caddis larva

10a. Case quite long (forty to seventy-five millimeters or more) and made of plant fragments in spiral or ring arrangement (fig. 5–20); top of middle and last thoracic segments lacking hard plates or with very minute plates: family Phryganeidae, nine genera, twenty-seven species (note: if case of spiral fragments, antennae prominent (fig. 5–21), and sickle-shaped plates on top of first and second thoracic segments, then genus *Triaenodes,* family Leptoceridae); abundant and widespread, especially in lakes and slow streams in vegetation; larvae slender and twenty-five to thirty-five or more millimeters in length; pale colored; emerge principally in spring and early summer; pupa swims rapidly to shore or emergent objects and crawls from water, usually hatch early morning or at night, fishing can be excellent with fly to imitate migrating pupa. Adults fourteen to forty millimeters; straw colored, light brown, mottled browns, grays, to bright oranges; antennae shorter than body; oviposit at surface or crawl under.

10b. Case variable but not composed of plant fragments arranged in distinct spiral pattern . . . 11

Fig. 5–20. Spiral case of Phryganeidae caddis larva

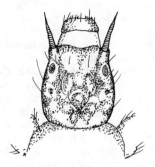

Fig. 5–21. Head of Leptoceridae caddis larva showing prominent antennae.

11a. Antennae quite prominent (fig. 5–21); hard plate on top of first and middle thoracic segments only; middle plate pale-colored and with two dark curved lines at sides; hind legs very long and heavily fringed with hair; case somewhat variable (silk tube, sand grains, plant fragments) but usually tapering and curved like a cornucopia, may have twigs fastened at side (fig. 5–22) or be ornamented with small shells: family Leptoceridae, seven genera, 101 species, *Nectopsyche* (formerly *Leptocella)* is the White Miller, *Mystacides* is the Black Dancer; widespread in lakes and streams, in vegetation and gravels; some larvae are strong swimmers; body thin, six to ten millimeters in length; straw to green colored; emerge all summer, crawl from water. Adults seven to seventeen millimeters long; black, white, or mottled; antennae extremely long, usually twice length of adult or more; adults mill about in erratic masses near bushes or over water; oviposit at film or crawl under.

11b. Antennae very small, hard to see even with hand lens ... 12

Fig. 5–22. Case of Leptoceridae caddis larva

12a. Antenna midway between eye and base of mandible (note: antenna very short, look closely with hand lens) (fig. 5–23); spacing hump on top of first abdominal segment often quite prominent (fig. 5–16); cases may be of the log cabin variety (fig. 5–19), composed of irregular bits of wood, linearly arranged grass fragments (fig. 5–24), or slender cylinders of stone or vegetable material with or without larger stones or long twigs at the sides (figs. 5–25 and 5–26): family

Limnephilidae, fifty-two genera, about 310 species; largest caddis family; most dwell in the colder waters of the northern tier and western states, preferring lakes or quiet river pools, although a few are found in swift waters; those in streams tend to have cases of pebbles, those in lakes tend to have cases of plant fragments; larvae eight to twenty-four millimeters long, variety of pale colors; emerge chiefly in summer and fall, often in evening or after dark, pupae of many species crawl or swim to shore; I have seen *Limnephilus* in lakes emerge in the film, members of other genera probably do also. Adults nine to twenty-five millimeters long; cream and brown mottled, mottled brown, dark brown, mottled gray and white, straw colored, yellowish brown, and rusty brown; antennae shorter than body; oviposit at water's surface or on vegetation at edge of or in water; this family is a very important one with many species that produce fishable hatches, it is especially significant on western lakes and streams; the Great Orange Sedge (*Dicosmoecus* spp.) is a very important October hatch in the West.

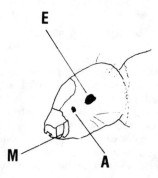

Fig. 5–23. Head of Limnephilidae caddis larva. Note antennae are very short. E, eye; M, mandible; A, antenna

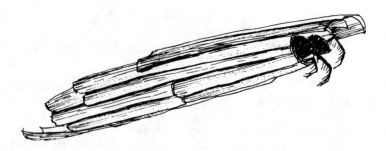

Fig. 5–24. Case of Limnephilidae caddis larva composed of linearly arranged plant fragments

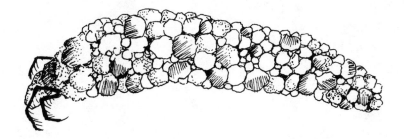

Fig. 5–25. Case of Limnephilidae caddis larva composed of pebbles

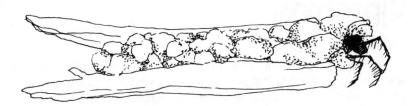

Fig. 5–26. Case of Limnephilidae caddis larva with twigs at sides

12b. Antennae located next to base of mandible, cases of sand grains or small pebbles, slightly curved and often slightly tapered: two families: (1) Odontoceridae, six genera, fourteen species; occur in streams across country; larvae eight and one-half to twenty millimeters long; pale green in color; larvae burrow deeply into gravels of bottom; pupate in clusters on underside of stones; spring and summer emergers, adults emerge rapidly in film. Adults six to sixteen millimeters long; mottled grays; antennae same length as body; oviposit at surface; this family is best known for eastern *Psilotreta*. (2) Family Sericostomatidae, three genera, twelve species; chiefly East and Midwest (genus *Agarodes);* in streams and lake edges; larvae may burrow; ten to thirteen millimeters long; pale colored; emerge in summer, rapidly at film. Adults mottled gray to brownish, six to ten millimeters long; antennae same length as body; oviposit in film.

6

Dipterans

There certainly is no scarcity of dipterans — over eight thousand species are known from North America alone! Most are terrestrial or pseudoaquatic (reproducing in temporary ponds or moist vegetation and soil), but many have true aquatic stages. Included in this large order of insects are deerflies, mosquitoes, gnats, midges, and craneflies. Possibly due to the diminutive size of many of the aquatic species, they are often overlooked by the angler; nonetheless, in terms of sheer numbers, this is frequently the most prevalent aquatic group. In slow streams and in ponds, the number of dipterans is astronomical, and even the very largest trout feed heavily on them. To the angler, the midges are of great significance, the craneflies, deerflies, and others of occasional importance.

All dipterans undergo complete metamorphosis. The larvae of aquatic species are wormlike and do not have true legs. They may have prolegs, soft, fleshy projections that are not jointed like true legs. Most dwell on the bottom, and imitations of these species should be weighted and drifted along the bottom. Some larvae, such as those of the mosquitoes, are agile swimmers and are best imitated by a twitching retrieve. Pupae of some species cement themselves to the bottom. Many, however, are free swimming and actively wiggle about. Adult dipterans may be easily recognized by the presence of only two wings; in fact, the name "Diptera" is formed of *di* meaning two and *ptera* meaning wing. The hind pair is reduced to two knob-shaped "halters" which help balance the insect during flight (fig. 5–6).

Egg laying habits are variable. Some dipteran females crawl just below the surface on logs, rocks, vegetation, or other objects. Others release their eggs at the surface or attach the eggs to objects just above the surface.

MIDGES

Most midges require less than a year to mature. In many instances, only a few weeks elapse between the time the eggs are deposited and the adults emerge. Through this rapid turnover of generations, the midges have evolved for the entire spectrum of freshwater habitats. They live in all lakes and streams, from the most disgustingly polluted, muck-bottomed sink holes to the purest, boulder-strewn mountain rivers. Where there is water, there are midges. And more midges. These insects usually make up fifty percent or more of all the species of invertebrates in any lake or stream. Add to their omnipresence and numbers the fact that they hatch every month of the year (provided there's open water), and you have a combination ready-made for the trout and the fly fisherman. Although midge populations are good in all waters, they are especially high in streams and lakes with silt bottoms and weed beds. In these areas they can reach densities far in excess of fifty thousand per square meter. It is little wonder that in such places they are a main component of the trout's diet.

Of the six families in this order that are usually called midges, the Chironomidae are of major significance to the angler (fig. 6–1). The other families can occasionally be important. As the name implies, these are small insects. Larvae vary from two to about thirty millimeters in length, and a large majority are less than ten. Like Joseph's coat, they come in many colors. Most common are blood red, brown, black, gray, and olive. Many species that burrow in bottom mucks, where oxygen levels are low, are red. These larvae are called bloodworms. The color is due to hemoglobin in their blood.

Larval imitations should stress the wormlike segmentation of the natural. Big midge larvae (ten to thirty millimeters) are not infrequently found in lakes and some streams. Polly Rosborough's Muskrat Nymph is an effective fish taker where these larger larvae live. Fish it dead drift on a long tippet or work it with a slow twitching retrieve near weed beds. Use a floating or sinking line as conditions dictate. For smaller larvae a Fur Midge Larva, a Midge Nymph, or George Harvey's Horse Collar Midge is excellent. The South Platte Brassy holds a special place in my heart for imitating midge larvae. Developed on and named after this famous Colorado River, this bare bones fly superbly imitates the brown and bloodred midge larvae. A bright copper wire body and a throat of feather fibers seem an unlikely fly, but the

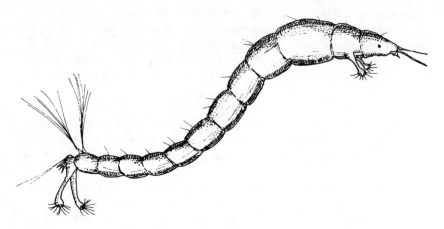

Fig. 6–1. A typical Chironomidae midge larva

trout accept it readily. Other colors of wire can be used to imitate other midge larvae.

Fishing the tiny larva imitations in streams is best accomplished if the angler can see the fish. Use a long, thin tippet so the fly can sink fast. Cast far enough above the fish that the imitation can get to its level before reaching it. Watch for the fish to turn its head or open its mouth as it takes the fly. These minute flies have made some astounding catches for me with this technique.

Blackfly larvae (family Simulidae, fig. 6–2) are one of the three principal components of behavioral drift (*Baetis* mayflies and scuds are the other two). Although behavioral drift is primarily nocturnal, some blackfly larvae drift during the day. Their habit of letting themselves out into the current by a silk thread attached to the bottom may contribute accidentally to high daytime drift rates; on the other hand, this habit may be an ingrained part of behavioral drift. Either way, the larvae are found floating free, and are therefore a target for trout. The Midge Nymph is a good imitation of these larvae. Fish it on a long tippet.

In spring ponds or in the shallows of lakes, trout can often be seen cruising in search of food. The trick to presenting a midge larva imitation to these fish is to cast far enough ahead of the trout so that the fly sinks to the fish's level a foot or two ahead of it. Angler-wise trout may refuse the sinking fly. In this case, cast the fly and allow it to settle to the bottom. Then, as the fish swims near, lift the rod tip to jump the fly off the bottom right in front of its nose. This trick has rarely failed.

In the deep, open water area of lakes, midge larvae rise to the surface just

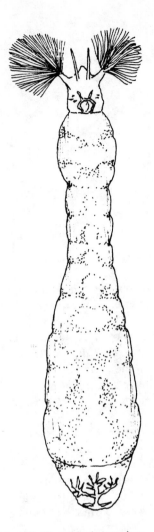

Fig. 6–2. Larva of the blackfly (Simulidae), top view

at dusk and remain high in the water all night, returning to the bottom at dawn. Trout cruise just under the surface taking the suspended larvae. A very effective technique is to fish the imitation on a greased leader (see below). Another tactic that is widely used in England employs a floating line and a long leader. The imitation is allowed to sink several feet, then the rod is raised *slowly* to pull the fly toward the surface. If no take occurs, the fly is allowed to sink and the process is repeated.

When the larva has matured, it pupates. Many fastwater species glue themselves to the bottom in special, silken chambers. Other midges have

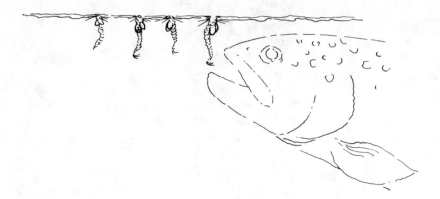

Fig. 6–3. Big fish will feed heavily when the midges are hatching.

freely swimming pupae. In the end the wormlike larva has changed so radically that it in no way resembles its former self. Inside the pupal skin an adult forms.

If the pupa is fastened to the bottom, emergence occurs underwater. The pupal chamber faces downstream (fig. 6–4). The adult pumps gasses around itself, explodes from the chamber, and pops to the surface in the bubble of gas. For these insects, a spider-type wet fly (silver tinsel body, black hackle) is excellent. Best sizes are #16 to #20. Fish them with plenty of action.

In those species most often encountered by the angler (family Chironomidae), the pupa has a thin, elongated, well-segmented abdomen and a short, robust thorax bearing down-curving wing pads and legs. Tufted, filamentous gills may be present on the thorax (fig. 6–5). While many of these Chironomidae midges are small (some are downright miniscule) others may be as much as twenty-five millimeters long. The larger pupae are

Fig. 6–4. Pupa of the blackfly (Simulidae)

Fig. 6–5. Typical pupa of Chironomidae midge

imitated very nicely by patterns similar to John Goddard's Hatching Midge Pupa. Medium-sized individuals are well matched with George Harvey's Horse Collar Midge. Tiny midge pupae can be aped quite well with the Midge Nymph.

Since Chironomidae pupae are free swimming, they can be fished successfully anytime. In lakes, the pupae often migrate from the bottom to the surface during the dark hours. As they wiggle around near the surface they become easy targets for cruising trout. Fish the fly on a floating line and greased leader, moving it slowly with a twitch, twitch, rest motion. During the day in lakes and streams, fish the fly around beds of vegetation and along the bottom with the same retrieve.

In the hours prior to a hatch, the pharate adults become restless. They rise a short way from the bottom or vegetation beds then settle back. This motion is repeated several times before they make the final ascent to emerge. Needless to say, the trout take advantage of the exposed insects.

During emergence these midges are in great peril; the pharate adult hangs vertically at the film — in plain view of any fish — while the adult struggles out of the pupal husk. Trout sip them in, leaving only a tiny dimple at the surface (called the smutting rise). Anglers often miss seeing the rises or assume they're made by chubs. The key to recognizing the midge hatch is to watch for the presence of adults. Frequently they form clouds as they emerge and hover over the water or along the shoreline. If you see the adults, watch for the characteristic dimpling rises. However, carefully analyze the situation before assigning all soft bulging rises to midge pupae, as the rise to terrestrials is similar at first glance. Look for the minute, cast pupal skins and the presence of adult midges before selecting a pattern. A surface screen is very helpful in finding cast pupal husks.

In addition, during the hatching period, the adults swarming just above the water may lead the angler to mistakenly think that trout are feeding on the adults, when in fact the fish are taking the pupae and emergers.

These seemingly frail insects emerge every month of the year, if there's open water. I've had surprisingly good fishing during midge hatches on sunny midwinter days.

Trout feeding on hatching midges may take pupae, emergers, stillborns, and adults, or they may concentrate with frustrating single-mindedness on only one stage. I have yet to find a positive way to rapidly determine which stage is being selected, but curiously enough, during any one hatch, nearly all the fish will be taking the same stage. It may have to do with the visibility or the availability of that stage. To determine the stage being taken I usually try several fish with imitations of each stage. The best first choice is a pupal imitation. Often, however, even the most realistic pupal imitation will be shunned. This occurs because the fish are selecting adults that are partially emergent, the insect haloed by the as-yet uncast pupal husk. Griffith's Gnat, described in Schwiebert's *Nymphs,* is a fine dressing to represent this emergent stage. Developed by George Griffith (one of the founders of Trout Unlimited), it is the finest imitation of emerging midges I've ever used. A peacock herl or dubbed fur body palmered with a tiny hackle feather completes the fly. For picky fish, Schwiebert recommends trimming the hackle top and bottom for a flush float. It's a trick that has made the day more than once. Tiny soft-hackle flies are also excellent emerger patterns.

If resting adults are being taken, a Micro-Poly-Caddis is most effective. When the flies return to oviposit, they may dance above the surface, dipping down to deposit their eggs. The rise to such insects is usually vigorous, small fish often leaping clear of the water in their excitement. In such instances a small-hackled pattern works well. I favor patterns such as those described in Ed Koch's *Fishing the Midge.* The tail is a few hackle fibers, the body is formed from tying thread, and the hackle is applied without wings.

Female Chironomidae can be larger and colored differently than the males. During mating, many males may cluster about one female and float along on the water. J. R. Harris describes this in his text *An Angler's Entomology,* and Bob Pelzl showed me this phenomenon on New Mexico's San Juan. Huge rafts of midges formed up along the sides of the river where the smaller, black males sought to fertilize the larger, olive females. As the milling clumps of insects drifted out into the currents, they quickly became fare for the trout. We tried several "mating swarm" flies of various materials, but had little success. Perhaps next time.

The female may also crawl beneath the surface and lay her eggs on the bottom structures. This is especially prevalent among the blackflies, and a black, spider-type wet fly is an excellent choice in such situations.

For fishing these flies, a long 7X or 8X tippet is essential to prevent the leader from bossing the fly and to decrease tippet visibility. Leaders needn't be excessively long; twelve feet is fine provided the tippet is at least three feet in length. To strike a fish on this fine material, simply raise the rod and *pull* the hook home. The small hook will catch in the skin of the trout's mouth and be very difficult to dislodge — a problem when releasing fish that can be overcome by debarbing the hook. Handling a big fish on the three-quarter- to one-pound tippets requires smooth, steady pressure from the rod with no jerking or sudden moves. Three- and four-weight rods in the eight- to nine-foot length work best for me. Make sure the reel has a smooth, light drag.

Fishing these minute imitations is not as difficult as it might seem. First, get as close as possible to the fish. This will allow greater accuracy and fly visibility. Then, use the greased leader tactic: Put paste floatant on the leader to within six inches of the fly. If you're fishing a pupal imitation, the greased leader will keep the fly riding just under the film like the naturals. When a fish takes the fly, the leader will draw under. If you're fishing an emerger or adult, the greased leader will make a track on the surface that you can use to locate your fly.

If you haven't fished for trout with midges, you've missed a special part of angling. Watch for them and give the mighty mites a try.

CRANEFLIES

These, the largest aquatic dipterans, also comprise the largest family of dipterans. Nearly fifteen hundred species of the Tipulidae family are known from North America alone. They resemble mosquitoes but are much larger (to sixty millimeters long) with narrow wings and extremely long, fragile legs that are easily lost. The adults are clumsy and fly only short distances.

The larvae of the aquatic species are large and wormlike, and are sometimes called waterworms. They live in all water types from ponds to rivers. Many species congregate in debris such as leaf packs along the shore. Others live in the gravels of swift riffles. In fact, there are few places they don't inhabit. They vary in color from dirty white to shades of brown, olive, and dingy orange. The exoskeleton of these larvae is often translucent with the viscera visible beneath. As pupation occurs in cells in the stream bank, this stage of the cranefly's life is not vulnerable to the trout.

For imitations of cranefly larvae, fur dubbing or fuzzy yarns, such as mohair, Mohlon, or the new sparkle yarns are superlative. For patterns of a more or less uniform color, wrap the shank with yarn and wind a rib of copper or silvered wire. Pick out the yarn slightly with a bodkin or scissor point. This shell of fibers gives the fly translucent, living coloration. Larvae that have a core of one color and outer tissues of a different color are simulated well by a coarsely dubbed body of a color to match the outer tissues, overwound with a rib of flat monofilament dyed to match the inner color of the larvae. The dubbing is then picked out to mimic the outer translucent layers. These flies should be weighted with fine lead wire wound under the body and fished dead drift along the bottom or worked very slowly on a sinking line. Cranefly larvae do occasionally swim; the body snaps back and forth like it was hinged in the center with a most peculiar, jerky motion. A Strip Leech or Maribou Streamer fished with a positive twitch is a good representation.

On western streams, and occasionally on eastern streams, good flights of craneflies do occur. The adults can be seen dancing above the water or moving about at the stream's edge. During such times a large skater-type dry fly can be fished with smashing results. Al Troth, an innovative fly tier from Dillon, Montana, described an excellent skater of elk hair in *Fly Tyer Magazine* (volume I, issue 3, 1978). It's tougher than hackle patterns and easy to tie (see appendix). This imitation is presented downstream or down and across. With the rod held high to keep the line off the water, the fly is skipped and bounced across the surface a few inches at a time. Line drag must be eliminated for best results; a greased leader will help immensely. And then, as Troth puts it: "I curl my toenails into the gravel awaiting the savage strikes this fly usually brings." Obviously, strong leaders are mandatory, 2X or 3X tippet at a minimum.

The methods are essentially those of Edward Ringwood Hewitt whose Neversink Skater — developed on his beloved Neversink River — is well known to eastern anglers. East or west, these patterns are not only deadly during periods when craneflies are about, but are often used to tease large fish into a savage rise during periods of little or no insect activity.

Due to their ponderous size and rangy structure, resting adult craneflies

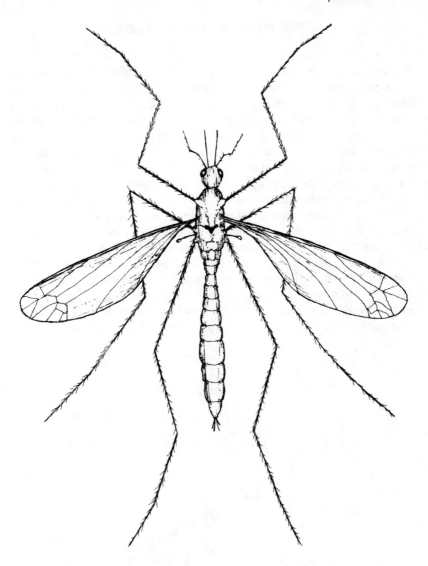

Fig. 6–6. Typical adult of cranefly (Tipulidae)

are difficult to imitate. Poul Jorgenson described a pattern in *Dressing Flies for Fresh and Salt Water* that was created by the famous Catskill fly tier Harry Darby. This is the best-looking pattern I've seen, but I have never used it since adult craneflies are seldom found resting on the surface.

DEERFLIES AND HORSEFLIES

About three hundred species of these insects from the Tabanidae family occur in the United States; many of them are semiaquatic. There are only three genera that have truly aquatic larvae, but they are widely distributed and common in freshwater systems. Most of the aquatic species are pond and swamp inhabitants, occupying the muddy shallows near the shore. Deerflies (genus *Tabanus),* however, prefer the swiftly running water of stream riffles. Eggs are laid just above the waterline on logs, rocks, or plants. When the larvae hatch, they drop into the water. Their bodies are cigar-shaped and strongly segmented. Prolegs are fleshy and knob-shaped, enhancing the segmented appearance. Larvae live one to three years, and at maturity are fifteen to forty millimeters long. They crawl out on shore, well above the water, and burrow into the ground to pupate. The biting adult horseflies and delta-shaped deerflies are known by all anglers.

As a miscellaneous component of trout stream fauna, the larvae are not of tremendous importance but in some streams, such as the San Juan in New Mexico, deerfly larvae can be extremely abundant, and thus, highly significant to the angler. In ponds, horsefly larvae can be surprisingly numerous. A Hair Leg Wooly Worm or a small version of the cranefly larvae is an effective imitation.

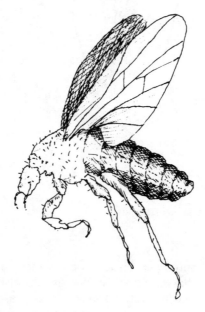

Fig. 6–7. The March Fly (Biblionidae)

Adults can be important during the summer days when no aquatic insects are hatching. A local, midwestern pattern called the Woodruff is fished back under the alders and along cedar snags with great success. It represents the deerflies very nicely. A Poly-Caddis of correct color is also a fine imitation.

Terrestrial dipterans, such as the housefly, can sometimes be important, but are, by and large, of passing interest to the angler. However, on eastern streams the adult March flies can be very important (fig. 6–7). These robust members of the family Bibionidae are six to ten millimeters long, ebony with scarlet, sometimes yellow, legs. They are seen in early spring when they fall or are blown in multitudes onto the water. I have seen fantastic numbers of March flies on such rivers as Pennsylvania's Bushkill and Broadheads. The silhouette of these insects is important in pattern development, the adults lying in the surface film with their wings often fully spent and pointing to the rear in a V position. The pattern I favor is dressed with a dubbed, black body; black poly wings tied delta style; and a scarlet or yellow thorax of dubbed material to suggest the legs. Though it is not a particularly handsome dressing, its effectiveness more than compensates for its looks.

Key to Diptera

This key to the larvae of the common aquatic Diptera includes notes on the larvae, pupae, and adults.

Larvae

1a. Larva of glasslike transparency with a dark air sac at each end, about thirteen millimeters long (fig. 6–8): family Chaoboridae, phantom midges; abundant in lakes, bogs, and spring ponds; good swimmers; migrate from bottom to surface at night. Pupae active swimmers. Adults emerge in the film; resemble mosquitoes but have hairy wings and do not bite; proboscis is very short; males with feathery antennae.

1b. Larva variously colored but not transparent . . . 2

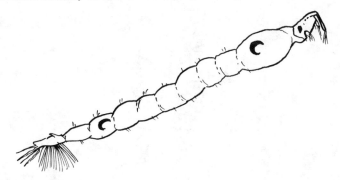

Fig. 6–8. A phantom midge larva (Chaoboridae)

2a. Larva seven-segmented with sucker on bottom of each of first six segments; four to twelve millimeters long (fig. 6–9): family Blephariceridae, one genus *Blepharicera*, net winged midges; attached firmly to rocks in fast water. Pupae attached to bottom; adults emerge under water. Adults have long legs and broad wings; wings have network of numerous fine lines; eyes with stripe dividing top and bottom.

2b. Larva not seven-segmented, or lacking suckers on bottom of first six segments . . . 3

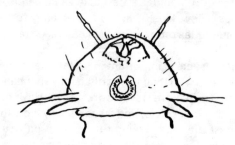

Fig. 6–9. Bottom view of head of net winged midge larva (Blephariceridae) showing sucker

3a. Abdomen with seven pairs of fleshy, lobed prolegs along the sides; larva about four millimeters long (fig. 6–10): family Deuterophlebiidae, one genus *Deuterophlebia*, mountain midges; creep slowly over rocks in clear mountain streams. Pupae adhere to bottom. Adults emerge underwater; wings are enormous and elaborately folded; males have very long, thin antennae.

3b. Abdomen of larva not as above . . . 4

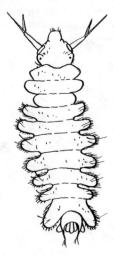

Fig. 6–10. Larva of mountain midge *(Deuterophlebia)*

4a. Last third of abdomen swollen and terminating in a disk used to attach larva to bottom; usually five millimeters long or less (range three to fifteen) (figs. 6–11 and 6–2): family Simulidae, blackflies; larvae attached to rocks in swift, shallow water. Pupae attached to bottom. Adults emerge underwater, have short, fat bodies; antennae very short; biting insects.

4b. Abdomen uniform in diameter or tapering rearward, not swollen at terminal end
... 5

Fig. 6–11. Side view of blackfly larva (Simulidae)

5a. Thoracic segments fused and larger in diameter than rest of body; three to fifteen millimeters long; (fig. 6–12): family Culicidae, mosquitoes; lakes and quiet water areas of streams. Pupae free swimming; biting insects

5b. Body more or less uniform in diameter from end to end, may be tapered at ends
... 6

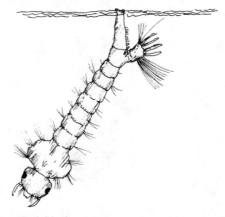

Fig. 6–12. Mosquito larva (Culicidae)

6a. Larvae pointed at both ends (cigar-shaped); fifteen to forty-four millimeters long, body robust and ringed with swollen fleshy prolegs (fig. 6–13): family Tabanidae, horseflies (lakes) and deerflies (streams). Pupate in soil on bank. Adults with heavy body; large insects; huge compound eyes; antennae very short; biting insects.

6b. Body of larva cylindrical and worm-shaped, not strongly cigar-shaped and without rings of prolegs . . . 7

Fig. 6–13. Larva of deerfly (Tabanidae)

7a. Abdomen ending in respiratory disk; head retractable into body; mouthparts closing horizontally; robust body distinctly segmented and nearly uniform in diameter from end to end; larva often very large, to seventy-five millimeters or more (fig. 6–14): family Tipulidae, craneflies; streams (riffles and pools) and lakes. Pupate in soil on bank. Adults look like huge mosquitoes; legs easily broken off; top of thorax with distinct V-shaped suture; head without simple eyes (ocelli) (fig. 6–6).

7b. Larva without retractable head and respiratory disk . . . 8

Fig. 6–14. Larva of cranefly (Tipulidae). H, head

8a. Larva with paired prolegs on first thoracic segment *and* last abdominal segment, head a sclerotized capsule, body thin and distinctly segmented, two to thirty millimeters; (figs. 6–15 and 6–1): family Chironomidae, midges; far and away the most important group to the fly fisherman, hundreds of species which occur in all fresh water systems, especially in areas of vegetation and muck; at least fifty species in any lake or stream; they may burrow in the bottom or crawl about in vegetation; all are active swimmers; lake dwelling species often migrate to surface at night. Pupae may remain in burrows of larvae or they may swim about in vegetation; emergence of adults is at the surface. Adults with long slender abdomen; wings narrow and significantly shorter than abdomen; top of last segment of thorax with furrow down the middle (fig. 6–16); males with plumed antennae.

8b. Paired prolegs absent from first thoracic segment and last abdominal segment; body of uniform diameter and bent into U-shape at rest (fig. 6–17); larva four to eight millimeters long: family Dixidae, dixa midges; lakes and slow water areas of streams near rocks and vegetation; larvae float at surface. Pupate out of water. Adults slender and retiring; long legs; antennae with short hairs.

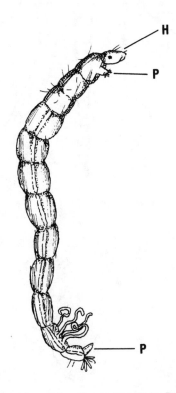

Fig. 6–15. Larva of Chironomidae midge. H, head capsule; P, proleg

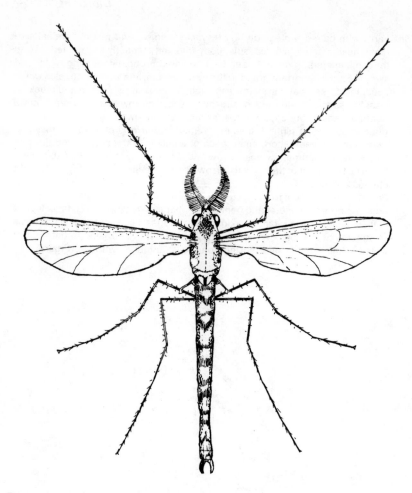

Fig. 6–16. Adult Chironomidae midge

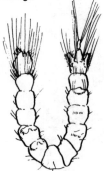

Fig. 6–17. Larva of dixa midge (Dixidae)

7

The Stillwater Insects

Only infrequently do any two ponds or streams have precisely the same assortment and distribution of organisms. However, in a broad sense, there are organisms associated more with lakes than with streams. Although not excluded from running water, most of the species in these groups occur in stillwater systems. Such is the case with the damselflies, dragonflies, and true bugs.

DAMSELFLIES AND DRAGONFLIES

The Odonata order is the oldest order of insects; its members were here to see the rise and fall of those great land leviathans, the dinosaurs. The Odonata, too, were big in those days. Fossils with twenty-seven-inch wingspans have been found. Today's versions are much smaller but are still sizable insects. This group includes over four hundred species in North America, and although most anglers readily recognize these insects, they are only vaguely aware of the importance of damselflies and dragonflies in the trout's diet. While the number of other food organisms may be greater than that of the Odonata nymphs, their robust size makes them a prized food item for even the largest trout.

Like mayflies and stoneflies, the Odonata have an incomplete life cycle. The egg produces a nymph that lives from several months to five years. Most

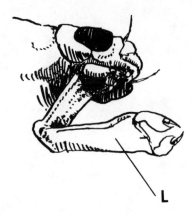

Fig. 7–1. Extensible labium of Odonata nymph. L, labium

species inhabit fresh water, although a very few are marine or are found in bogs and temporary ponds. The nymphs are voracious predators, feeding on midge and caddis larvae, nymphs of mayflies and stoneflies, trout fry and other small fishes, and under crowded conditions even one another. The lower jaw (labium) of the Odonata nymph is superbly engineered for its predacious existence. It is broad, greatly elongated (often to one-fourth of the body length), and hinged like the boom of a steam shovel. At the end are two toothed and spined scoops that snare the prey as the jaw unfolds and snaps forward (fig. 7–1). The *odus* in "Odonata" means tooth, and refers to these strong-toothed mouthparts. These rapacious nymphs may prowl about in the vegetation carefully stalking their quarry or lie buried in the bottom detritus to shoot forward and snare their victims. Once the prey is ensnared, the jaw folds back against the face to form a basket in which the food is held to be eaten at leisure.

At maturity, the nymph crawls from the water onto the bank, reeds, or boulders. As the nymphal husk dries, it splits between the shoulders and the adult emerges. First the thorax and head are pulled out. These are followed by the legs and wings, and finally, the abdomen. The newly emerged adult is soft and pale yellow. When its wings have expanded and dried, this "teneral" adult flies awkwardly to the protective cover of nearby vegetation. Strong winds during the emergence period often dash the tenerals to the water. Trout seize them readily. I've also seen fish leap from the water to pick the tenerals from grass overhanging a stream.

After a day or two the body hardens and takes on full coloration. The adult then flies away in pursuit of mosquitoes and other insects. Although too

Fig. 7–2. Mating position of Odonata adults

closely set for walking, the legs are well adapted for capturing flying insects. The front ones are bristled and form a basket against the sternum where the prey is trapped. The meal is eaten as the dragonfly or damselfly hovers in the air. To rest, these insects perch on objects near the water. Adults live several weeks to several months.

Almost without exception, adults are on the wing only during sunny periods of the day and then only in sunlit areas. If a cloud should momentarily cover the sun, they disappear as if by magic. So strong is the instinct for flying in sunlight, that during prolonged periods of inclement weather, whole populations may starve to death. A notable exception is the dragonfly *Neurocordulia yamaskanensis* which is wholly an evening flier that feeds on *Hexagenia* mayflies.

Mating occurs near the water. First, the male deposits a sperm packet in a special chamber on the underside of his second or third abdominal segment. When he finds a mate, he grasps her head or the fore part of the thorax with the claspers on the end of his abdomen. She then folds forward under the male and takes the sperm into the end of her abdomen (fig. 7–2). Once the eggs are fertilized, the couple may fly in tandem, the male still holding onto the female, and oviposit, or they may separate, in which case the male remains nearby during egg laying.

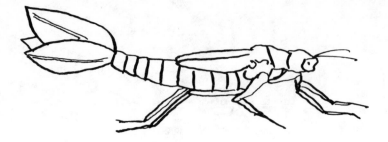

Fig. 7–3. A typical damselfly nymph showing three paddle-shaped gills

Damselflies

Damselfly nymphs can be easily recognized. Three paddle-shaped gills occur at the end of the long, slender abdomen. The short, husky thorax bears the wing pads and long, rangy legs (fig. 7–3). The head is short, but with the bulging compound eyes it is wider than the thorax. Nymphal color varies, not only from species to species, but to some degree for any individual. The body color can change somewhat to more closely match the substrate. Most nymphs are shades of olive, olive brown, tan, or purplish brown. Overall size ranges from fifteen to thirty millimeters. They are the denizens of ponds, small lakes, and the quiet water of streams and large lakes across the United States. They are especially prevalent in western lakes. Damsel nymphs are crawlers or swimmers, searching for food near aquatic plants and bottom debris.

Most damselflies have a one-year life cycle, but in the very abundant and widespread genera *Enallagma* and *Ischnura,* there can be two or more broods per summer. At maturity, the nymphs leave the protection of the vegetation or bottom debris and head for shore, swimming just under the surface. Such migration usually occurs on sunny mornings, but may extend into the early afternoon hours. They move by undulating their bodies back and forth like minnows, aided by paddlelike gills. The nymph swims a foot or so then stops and rests for a few moments before repeating. The legs are held out to the sides as the organism swims. The wiggle must be most provocative to the trout, for the fish frequently roll and splash as they rush to grab the migrating nymphs. The actual date of hatching varies with the species and with elevation and latitude. Generally speaking, June and July are the prime months to experience the damselfly emergence.

The adults have long, slender abdomens. The fore wings and hind wings are equally wide, and in many species, their bases are strongly pinched or stalked (fig. 7–8), giving the appearance of a yoke. *Zygo* meaning yoke has given the damselfly suborder its name: Zygoptera. At rest most species hold the wings slanting back along the top of the abdomen (fig. 7–4). Eyes are large and separated by a distance greater than the diameter of one eye, which distinguishes the damsels from the dragons (whose eyes touch or nearly touch on top of the head). Damselfly adults are twenty-five to fifty millimeters long. Males are often bright: emerald with black wings, bright blue with clear wings, red with red wing bases, and so on. Females are usually dull colored: olives, browns, tans, pale yellow, and others.

Eggs are injected into the submerged portions of aquatic plants. The male retains his mating hold on the female and the two of them fly in tandem to a weed bed. In most species, the male lands on a weed and lowers the female partially or wholly beneath the surface. The common Black-Winged Damsel *(Calopteryx maculata)* that inhabits streams in the eastern United States is an exception. The male releases the female when they arrive at a suitable egg laying site. She then crawls beneath the surface to deposit eggs in submerged plants. After ovipositing, the female floats to the surface some distance downstream where she is picked up by the male. The well-known English angler and author John Goddard says that this latter method of egg laying is the only one he has observed for damsels in the lakes of Great Britain.

Either way, this is a dangerous time for the adults. Being, at best, fitful fliers, they are easily blown about by the wind, and often are cast onto the water's surface. Trapped in the film, they struggle weakly. The fore wings are outstretched like the spent wings of a mayfly. The hind wings lie flush in the film but pointed back along the abdomen in an inverted V. Trout feed on the mired insects with deliberate head and tail rises. Females that crawl

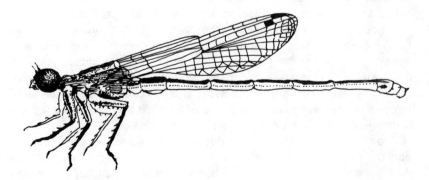

Fig. 7–4. Typical damselfly adult

beneath the surface are taken as they clamber about and as they float back to the surface.

Damselfly imitations must stress the size, color, and silhouette of the stage being taken by the trout. Nymphs should be designed to actively swim and should stress the slender abdomen, thick thorax, and obvious legs of the natural. Adults should have a long, slender body, one pair of out-stretched wings, and one pair of delta-shaped wings, and should lie flat in the film. Patterns of this type are given in the appendix.

Once the life cycle of these organisms is understood, angling tactics become obvious. In lakes and the quiet water of streams, the nymph can be fished at the edges of weed beds or deep along the bottom on a sink tip or full sinking line. Move the fly slowly a few inches, let it rest, and repeat the entire sequence. When the nymphs are migrating to shore, fish from the shore so that your fly is moving the same direction as the naturals. Use a floating line and long leader with a three- or four-foot tippet. Apply a paste floatant to the butt of the leader; this will hold the fly just under the surface. Move the artificial about a foot with a hand-twist retrieve and two or three *small* twitches of the rod tip. Let the fly sit still for several seconds and repeat. Trout often pick up the nymph when it's stopped, so watch for the greased leader butt to twitch and signal a take.

If the trout can be seen, pitch the fly several feet ahead of him so it has a chance to sink to its level. Watch for the white flash of the fish's mouth as it takes the fly. Angler-wise trout may reject the sinking nymph. I once located such a fish during a damselfly hatch on a western lake. Each time I would show him the nymph, he would shy away. I finally cast the artificial far ahead of him and allowed it to sink and rest on the bottom. When the fish cruised near the fly, a lift of the rod jumped the nymph off the bottom. He took it confidently. In the net, the reason for the trout's caution became apparent. One of the bony plates along the outer edge of the upper jaw was missing, probably torn away during an encounter with another angler.

The adults can provide spectacular dry fly fishing, as Bob Pelzl and I found out one July. We were fishing the lakes on the Vermejo Park Ranch in northeastern New Mexico and in the bright sun of midday encountered a huge flight of ovipositing damsels. The brilliant blue *Ischnura* were all around us, along the weeds and in the flooded timber. Gusting winds were constantly tossing them onto the water. Our fly boxes were woefully lack-ing, but big hair wing spinners of the Giant Michigan Mayfly *(Hexagenia limbata)* were a close enough match to the females. Bob's four-pound rainbow topped a long list of big trout we took in three hours of extraordi-nary dry fly fishing. These fish had nymphs in the lower stomach (taken during the morning's migration to shore) and adults in the upper stomach and gullet.

From our observations of the naturals that afternoon, we developed the Hair-Wing Damsel. It proved to be an extremely effective fly when fished dead on the surface or twitched occasionally to excite a cautious fish. Our good friend, Ed Roe, from Santa Fe, also found it killing when twitched along just beneath the surface.

Key to Damselflies

This key to the nymphs of the damselfly families (order Odonata, suborder Zygoptera) includes notes on adults and selected genera.

1a. First segment of antenna as long or longer than total length of remaining segments; outer two gills (tails) triangular in cross section: family Calopterygidae, broad-winged damselflies, stream insects, two genera, eight species; wings of adult are gradually narrowed rather than stalked (fig. 7–5); this family includes the largest damsels (body length to fifty, wingspan to eighty millimeters). *Calopteryx maculata (Agrion maculatum)* is the well-known black-winged, metallic-green-bodied damsel of the eastern United States. *Hetaerina americana* is the widespread and common American Ruby Spot; the body and wing bases are red.

1b. First segment of antenna similar in length to second segment; outer two gills flattened in cross section . . . 2

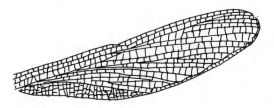

Fig. 7–5. Wing of broad-winged damselfly adult (Calopterygidae)

2a. Gills of nymph heavily thickened and darkly colored on basal half, thin and not colored on apical half (fig. 7–6): family Protoneuridae; two genera, two species; restricted to streams in Texas

2b. Gills not thickened and darkened on basal half . . . 3

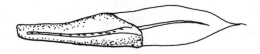

Fig. 7–6. Gill of Protoneuridae damselfly nymph. Note thickened basal portion.

3a. Gills of nymph with many small, mostly unbranched veins arising at right angles to the large central vein (fig. 7–7): family Lestidae, spread-winged damselflies; two genera, eighteen species; lake and stream insects; wings of adult are stalked at base (fig. 7–8); at rest, body is held vertically and wings are spread like a dragonfly's. Species of *Lestes* inhabit marshy edges of lakes and streams across the United States; adults have clear wings and yellowish to green bodies mottled with black. *Archilestes* is a western genus that inhabits stream edges; colored similarly to *Lestes.*

3b. Small veins of gills highly branched, diverge from central vein at much less than right angles (fig. 7–9): family Coenagrionidae, narrow-winged damselflies; fifteen genera, ninety-three species; lake and stream insects; wings of adult narrow and stalked at base; at rest, wings are held together and back over top of body. *Enallagma* and *Ischnura* are blue-colored insects found in all areas; they are especially abundant in western lakes. The Violet Dancer *(Argia violacea)* is a common violet-colored species found near streams and ponds.

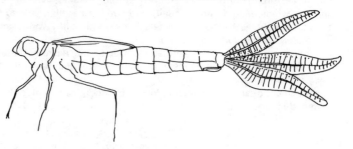

Fig. 7–7. Nymph of spread-winged damselfly (Lestidae) showing veins in tracheary gills

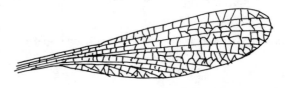

Fig. 7–8. Stalked damselfly wing

Fig. 7–9. Tracheary gills of narrow-winged damselfly showing veination

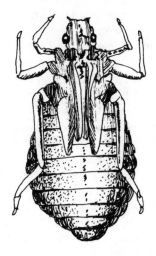

Fig. 7–10. A typical dragonfly nymph

Dragonflies

Dragonfly nymphs are large, squat monsters that may attain a length of forty-five millimeters. The abdomen is usually short, wide, and flattened top and bottom (fig. 7–10). Their internal gills are in a rectal chamber. Strong abdominal muscles draw in and expel water from the chamber to aerate the gills; the nymph is jet-propelled by a sharp contraction of these muscles. Dragonfly nymphs are dull gray, olive, brownish, to blackish in color and most frequently occur in slow streams or in ponds. However, several species in the families Gomphidae and Cordulegastridae inhabit gravelled riffles and rapids. I have found these insects in streams across the country. In Wisconsin's Namekagon River, for example, these active-water nymphs are one of the basic foodstuffs of the trout, the fish growing rapidly on this diet of large nymphs.

Nymphal habits vary greatly. The Aeshnidae are climbers, prowling in vegetation and bottom debris. Libellulidae and Macromiidae are long legged sprawlers that squat immobile on many types of bottoms. The Cordulegastridae snuggle down into the gravel of riffles by raking out a depression. Petaluridae and Gomphidae burrow into the bottom, leaving only the eyes and tip of the abdomen showing.

Dragonfly nymphs live one to four years, and trout are able to find them year round. These big insects are especially significant in the winter months, when insects with a one-year life cycle are small and provide little food for trout. A good concentration of the big Odonata nymphs can mean prime winter conditions. Imitations can be successful any time of the year, but are especially effective in early spring and late fall. Charlie Brooks's Assam Dragon is a strongly impressionistic fly that could represent many large, juicy organisms. Carey's Special and the Muskrat are also good imitations of dragonfly nymphs. The Fur Chenille Dragon represents the form of the nymph more closely and has been a good fly for me.

In ponds and the slow water of streams the large, streamer-sized nymphal imitations may be twitched slowly along the bottom and among weed beds. Use a sinking line and count the seconds required for the line to reach bottom. Then, on the next cast, fish the fly just off the bottom, starting the retrieve a few seconds before the line is completely settled. These nymphs can also be fished with a rapid start-stop retrieve to imitate their jet-propelled movements. Charlie Brooks counts this among the most successful methods for large trout in the region around Yellowstone Park. It is effective anywhere these nymphs occur.

In fast water, I often fish the nymphs in tandem on a fifty-inch leader and high density line, pinching microshot on the leader to get the flies down quickly and keep them down (fig. 7–11). The cast is made across and upstream, and as the line sinks and bellies out, the rod lifts and follows through high, providing maximum sensitivity to the strike. Heavy tippets (six to ten pounds) are essential since the take of the big fish against the drag of the sinking line is devastating.

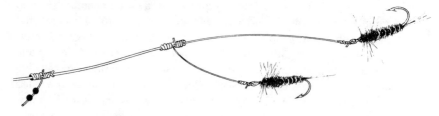

Fig. 7–11. A system for fishing two flies and split shot

Emergence occurs at night or in early morning during the spring and summer. Adult dragonflies are large, robust insects with huge compound eyes that meet or nearly meet on top of the head. Like the damsels, they frequently are brilliantly colored. At rest, the wings stretch out horizontally (fig. 7–12). They are powerful and graceful fliers, so strong that swarms of sexually immature insects often migrate great distances, one report indicating movement from Spain to Ireland. Superb hunters, they prowl the

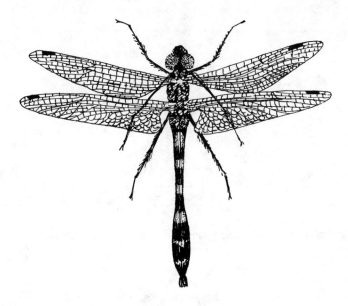

Fig. 7–12. Dragonfly adult

edges of watercourses searching for other insects such as caddises, moths, bees, even other, smaller species of Odonata. The suborder's name, "Anisoptera," refers to their wide hind wings and narrow fore wings *(aniso means unequal)*.

Eggs may be deposited in a number of ways. Members of the family Cordulegastridae hover above shallow water and thrust their abdomens down to the bottom. The Aeshnidae and Petaluridae deposit their eggs in aquatic plants. Others release eggs into the water by repeatedly touching the tip of the abdomen to the surface. Trout will jump for the hovering adults, but I have never found them to be as significant as damsel adults.

Key to Dragonflies

Identification of dragonfly nymphs, even to the family level, requires careful examination of the extensible labium (fig. 7–13). Simply unfold it from underneath the insect and observe it with a hand lens. Adults are keyed on the basis of wing veins. For adult keys see Merritt and Cummins (1978) and Walker (1953).

1a. Prementum (fig. 7–13) of extensible labium cupped, when folded back under the body the prementum covers the lower face of the insect up to the base of the antennae (fig. 7–14) . . . 2

1b. Prementum of extensible labium flat and does not cover face . . . 4

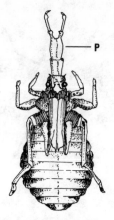

Fig. 7–13. Typical dragonfly nymph with labium extended. P, prementum

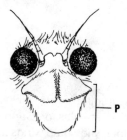

Fig. 7–14. Cupped prementum (P) covering face of nymph

2a. Two lobes at end of prementum with coarse and irregular teeth (fig. 7–15): family Cordulegastridae, one genus *Cordulegaster,* biddies, seven species; the nymphs are common inhabitants of the gravel areas of small woodland streams; they scoop a pit in the bottom to sprawl in. Adults are large and yellowish strongly marked with blackish brown; they fly slowly a foot or two above the water.

2b. Lobes at end of prementum with even and regular teeth or lacking teeth . . . 3

Fig. 7–15. Lobes of prementum with irregular teeth *(Cordulegaster)*

3a. Insect with prominent horn that sticks up between antennae: family Macromiidae, belted skimmers, two genera, eleven species; nymphs are found in ponds and streams where they sprawl in bottom sediments. Adults are extremely fast fliers; brown to brown with prominent yellow markings; eyes are bright green.

3b. Insect without upright horn but with flat shelf that extends forward between antennae: families Libellulidae, common skimmers, twenty-eight genera, ninety-one species and Corduliidae, green eyed skimmers, eight genera, forty-nine species; nymphs of these two families are not easily separated. Libellulidae is the largest family of dragonflies; nymphs are nearly all confined to ponds and lakes, only six or so species inhabit streams (slow water); many crawl about in vegetation, others sprawl in sediments. Adults vary widely in size but most are large (to seventy-five millimeters); wings are frequently spotted or banded; flight is erratic; body often brightly colored. Corduliidae inhabit bogs, ponds, and springs; they are sprawlers and climbers. Adults are blackish and often have a metallic sheen; eyes are brilliant green; flight consists of alternating periods of movement and hovering.

4a. Ends (tarsi) of foreleg and middle leg with two segments each (fig. 7–16): family Gomphidae, clubtails, fourteen genera, eighty-six species; mostly stream inhabitants, nymphs occur in riffles and slow water, burrow into bottom. Bodies of adults yellow to pale green and mottled with dark bands; they usually land on bare horizontal surfaces (unlike most dragonflies which perch with the body held vertical); the tail end of the abdomen is frequently much enlarged (fig. 7–12). The two largest genera, *Gomphus* and *Ophiogomphus,* are riffle dwellers in streams of all sizes.

4b. Middle tarsus with three distinct segments . . . 5

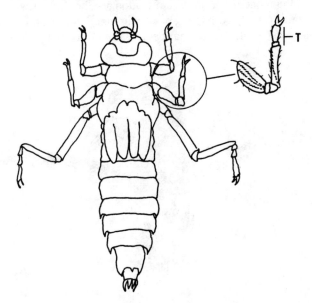

Fig. 7–16. Gomphidae dragonfly nymph. Note two-segmented tarsus (T).

5a. Antennae thick, segments short and hairy: family Petaluridae, graybacks, two genera, two species; nymphs inhabit small streams in wooded valleys; they burrow into the bottom. Adults are gray to blackish and often rest on tree trunks.

5b. Antennae thin, like a bristle: family Aeshnidae, darners, eleven genera, thirty-seven species; nymphs inhabit ponds and slow water areas of streams; they crawl about in vegetation or sprawl in bottom sediments. Adults are largest and strongest fliers of all dragonflies; many are marked with blues and greens.

TRUE BUGS

Trout in lakes do not hold in one spot; rather they cruise searching for food. One day, splashes in the weedy shallows along a shore indicated a school of trout had moved in and were feeding heavily. Cattails hid my approach, and as I waded cautiously to the outer edge of the stand, swarms of backswimmers sculled ahead of me in their peculiar, jerky way. The first cast confirmed my suspicion that the trout were hunting these insects. For two months I fished the pond, taking trout every trip on these hemipterans. Don't overlook this group. They are transcontinental and inhabit most ponds and lakes and the quiet water along the banks of streams.

Along with many terrestrials, the order Hemiptera includes aquatic species such as the water boatman, backswimmer, water scorpion, giant waterbug, water strider, and others. The name "Hemiptera" refers to the thickened basal half of the fore wings *(hemi,* half; *ptera,* wings). To the fisherman, the most important aquatic bugs are the dark brown to grayish water boatman (family Corixidae), backswimmer (family Notonectidae), and giant waterbug (family Belostomatidae). Water boatmen (fig. 7–17) average

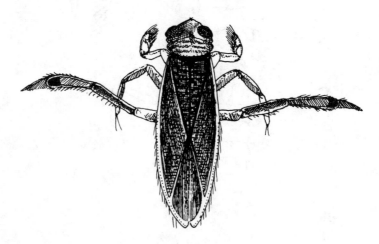

Fig. 7–17. A water boatman (Corixidae)

seven millimeters in length and the larger backswimmers about fifteen millimeters. Backswimmers (fig. 7–18) take their name from their habit of swimming upside down. Giant waterbugs are just that: giant. They range in size from eighteen to seventy millimeters or more, most are fifty to seventy long (fig. 7–19).

All have a gradual metamorphosis. There is an egg, a true nymph, and an adult. The true nymph looks like the adult, but is smaller and lacks fully developed wings. With each molt, the wings increase in size. The hind legs of these insects are long, flattened, and fringed for swimming. Tubular, piercing mouthparts are well developed in the backswimmers and giant waterbugs and can inflict a painful bite. In some areas the giant waterbugs are called toe-biters. The tubular mouthparts are used to pierce other insects, small fishes, and tadpoles and draw out their body juices. Mouthparts of the water boatman are broadly triangular rather than tubular. They feed on algae, minute animals such as rotifers, and small midge larvae.

Aquatic bugs must breathe gaseous oxygen. They carry a bubble of air with them when they dive. In well-oxygenated water, the gas exchange occurs at the interface between the bubble and the water, the bugs remaining submerged indefinitely. Most bugs renew their air supply by poking the terminal end of the abdomen above the surface. Some water boatmen poke the top of the thorax through the film. At rest, these bugs hang head down just under the surface with their tail ends sticking through the surface. Trout readily sip these resting bugs from the film. An imitation fished on a greased leader is highly effective.

Air entrapped around the body so greatly increases its buoyancy that the insect must swim or attach itself to the bottom in order to stay submerged. Its body glistens like silver as it darts through the water. Patterns of blended sparkle yarn coarsely dubbed and ribbed with silver tinsel are highly effective in imitating these insects. Stress the jerky swimming motion when fishing them.

Aquatic bugs overwinter as adults and can be surprisingly active even under the ice. It's a little-known fact that the giant waterbugs migrate to streams to overwinter. They buzz as they fly and hit the water with a definite splat. There can be some exciting angling when these bugs are on the move. Ben Egger used to hunt the locations of large trout in the fall in preparation for the flights of giant waterbugs. He always took good fish when these insects were migrating.

Other aquatic hemipterans include the creeping waterbugs, (family Naucoridae), water scorpions (family Nepidae), and water striders (family Gerridae). These figure so infrequently in the trout's diet that it would be next to useless to carry imitations of them.

Of the many terrestrial bugs, the jassids (leafhoppers, fig. 7–20) are by far

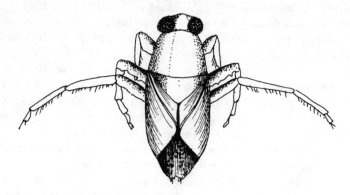

Fig. 7–18. A backswimmer (Notonectidae)

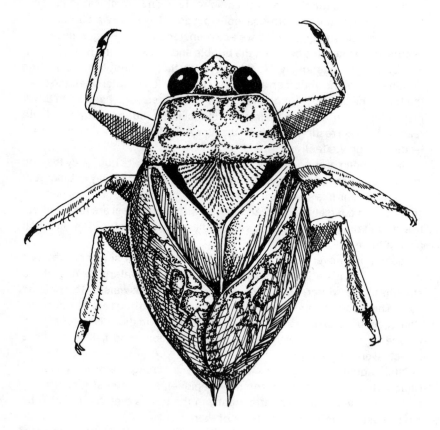

Fig. 7–19. A giant waterbug (Belostomatidae)

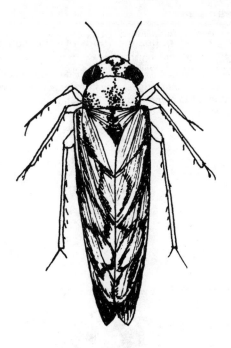

Fig. 7–20. A jassid

the most important to the fisherman. These trihedron insects range from three millimeters to more than twelve millimeters in length and come in a whole spectrum of colors. Jassids are powerful jumpers and on windy days are often carried onto the water, especially in open meadow areas, where trout rise freely to this diminutive fare.

Vince Marinaro has convincingly shown that silhouette is the most important feature of jassid imitations. Silhouette consists not only of the shape and size of the insect, but also the manner in which the insect depresses the surface film. Unless it is within the trout's window, all the fish sees of the insect is a sparkling depression in the mirror-like undersurface of the water. The shape of this depression is specific for each type of insect and is the trout's first clue that food is on its way. Thus, the artificial must sit in the surface in the same manner as the natural. Marinaro's Jungle Cock Jassids did just that. Since the publication of Marinaro's work, importation of jungle cock has been banned, and fly tiers have switched to other materials such as lacquered feathers to tie the tiny imitations. The Poly-Beetle is also a fine representation of the jassids.

Key to Aquatic Bugs

The following key identifies the adults of some common aquatic bugs.

1a. Beak broad, blunt, and triangular (fig. 7–21); tarsus of front leg and one-segmented scoop (fig. 7–17): family Corixidae, water boatmen. Pond dwellers that also occur at stream edges, they fly to large rivers and lakes to overwinter.

1b. Beak cylindrical and elongated (fig. 7–22); tarsus of foreleg not scoop-shaped and with several segments . . . 2

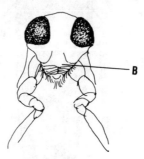

Fig. 7–21. Underside of head of water boatman (Corixidae). Note blunt, triangular beak (B).

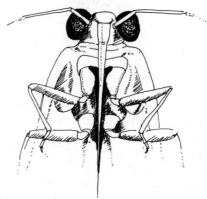

Fig. 7–22. Beak of bug modified for sucking

2a. Insect less than sixteen millimeters long, body flattened (fig. 7–18); insect swims upside down: family Notonectidae, backswimmers. Live in ponds and lakes with emergent vegetation; predators; dispersed widely.

2b. Large insects (over eighteen, usually forty to sixty millimeters) (fig. 7–19): family Belostomatidae, giant waterbugs. Fierce predators that live in ponds and lakes; fly to streams to overwinter.

8

Wooly Worm Larvae

While adapting plants and animals for every conceivable environment, nature's subtle experiments in evolution sometimes produce similar features in widely unrelated organisms. So it is with the wooly worm larvae. These lookalike insects belong to three orders: Megaloptera, Coleoptera, and Lepidoptera. Their silhouettes are so much alike that only one pattern is needed to successfully imitate all of them, and no matter where you fish, it's highly probable that one or more of these larvae will be found. This widespread presence is one of the reasons for the success of the Wooly Worm fly. Overall, in any one watershed, these insects would be labelled common but not highly abundant. However, the large size and year-round presence of many of these larvae make them a choice tidbit for even the biggest trout, another good reason why the Wooly Worm is such a productive pattern.

These insects are widely distributed throughout the United States. The dull colored adults are seen in spring and summer flying clumsily near streams and lakes where the larval stages occur. Metamorphosis is complete. Eggs are deposited on the underside of vegetation or other objects overhanging the stream or lake, and upon hatching, the larvae drop into the water. They live in riffles or in the bottom accumulations of backwater areas

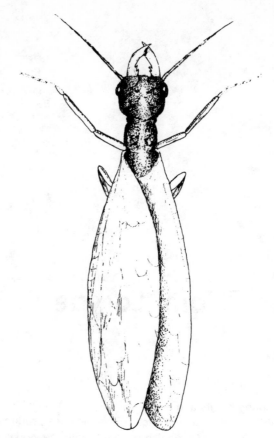

Fig. 8–1. Adult, female dobsonfly *(Corydalus)*

in streams and near the shorelines of lakes. Fierce predators, they attack and feed on all types of aquatic organisms, especially other insects. As they crawl or occasionally snake around on the bottom, they are easy prey to the trout. Pupation requires one to two weeks and occurs in dirt cells on the bank. Adults emerge to live for only a few days. If they alight or are blown onto the water, these big insects are readily seized by the trout.

The order Megaloptera *(megalo,* large; *ptera,* wing) is divided into two families: Corydalidae, embracing the dobsonflies and fishflies; and Sialidae or alderflies. Dobsonflies and fishflies are North American insects, and of the twenty known species, the dobsonflies are the largest. The adult has a wingspread of 100 to 150 millimeters (fig. 8–1). These grayish insects are nocturnal, spending the evening and night hours mating and egg laying. In the daytime, dobsonflies rest on vegetation near the water. Both male and female have sizable mandibles. Those of the male Eastern Dobsonfly are

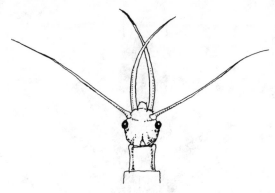

Fig. 8–2. Head of adult, male dobsonfly *(Corydalus)* showing huge tusklike mandibles

extremely long and tusklike, (fig. 8–2) and as the insect flies about, it nervously clashes them open and closed. An encounter with a large flight of these gigantic insects in the gray vagueness of late evening is not soon forgotten. The male of the infrequently encountered Pacific Dobsonfly lacks the tusklike mandibles. There are five genera of fishflies. Adults are similar in shape to, and have strong mandibles like, the dobsonflies, but are smaller, with wingspans ranging from 40 to 75 millimeters. Some are noc-

Fig. 8–3. Adult Black Fishfly *(Nigronia)*

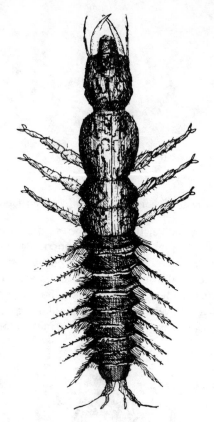

Fig. 8–4. The hellgrammite (larva of dobsonfly, *Corydalus*)

turnal but others, like the Black Fishfly, (fig. 8–3) are frequently seen on sunny days flying awkwardly near the water. Dobsonflies and fishflies resemble stoneflies, both at rest and in flight. However, the large mandibles of the Corydalidae and the somewhat spread and tent-shaped position of the wings at rest serve to separate these insects from the stoneflies.

In streams, dobsonfly and some fishfly larvae characteristically inhabit riffles and stony runs. Some fishflies prefer eddies where dead leaves and sticks accumulate. They require two or three years to fully develop. At maturity they are fifty to ninety millimeters long and usually deep brown to blackish. Their first eight abdominal segments bear long lateral filaments, and the mandibles are well developed, as anyone who has collected this excellent trout and bass bait can attest. Hellgrammites (or dobsonfly larvae) are distinguished by the presence of tufted gills at the base of each lateral filament, a feature the fishfly larvae lack (figs. 8–4, 8–5).

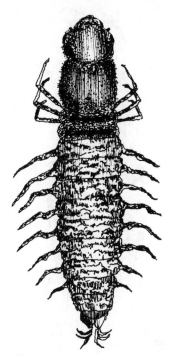

Fig. 8–5. Fishfly larva

Alderflies are distributed across Europe and North America and have long been recognized by British anglers as an important hatch. Adults of the twenty-three North American species are uniformly brownish gray and average ten to fifteen millimeters in length. The alder looks like a husky caddisfly (fig. 8–6) and was given its common name in England where large flights fill the streamside shrubs. These insects prefer the sunlight and are often seen ovipositing during midday.

Alderfly larvae require one or two years to mature. They are twenty to thirty-five millimeters long and a mottled brownish color. In streams they commonly inhabit gravel and backwater eddies where debris accumulates. There are only seven pairs of abdominal filaments on these larvae, and they have a single, tail-like, terminal filament which is lacking in the hellgrammites and fishfly larvae (fig. 8–7). In addition, the mandibles of the alderflies are not as prominent as those of the dobsonflies and fishflies. Trout fishermen will most frequently encounter the larvae of the alderflies and the fishflies; hellgrammites are usually found in warmer water more suited to bass.

Fishfly and alderfly larvae are common but never as numerous as mayfly nymphs and some other insects. However, the sheer size of these

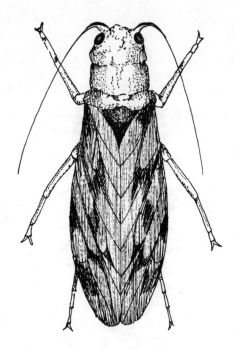

Fig. 8–6. Adult alderfly (Sialidae)

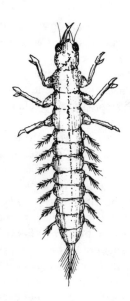

Fig. 8–7. Larva of alderfly (Sialidae)

Megaloptera larvae makes them a highly caloric item on the trout's menu. Also, because the larvae of many species live more than one year, they are an especially valuable source of trout food during the cold months when hatches are minimal and many other immature insects are very small. In the early spring, the maturing larvae are active, having a final growth spurt in preparation for pupal metamorphosis. This is probably their most vulnerable period. Increased activity and growth precipitates drift, and as the big larvae tumble out of the riffles and into the pools below, they become fodder for the waiting trout. It pays to determine if these insects occur in the waters you expect to fish.

Although the standard Wooly Worm with its peacock herl, dubbed fur or yarn body, and palmered hackle imitates these larvae well, I prefer a Hair-Leg Wooly Worm tied with a mohair body and hair legs. Mohair's natural translucency, wide range of colors, ease of dyeing with commercial fabric dyes when necessary, and fuzziness make it a most appealing material. Because hair legs are bulkier than hackle, I prefer them on many patterns.

In early spring, it pays to spend the hatchless days probing the bottom with a pair of big flies such as these. Fishing the large Wooly Worms in streams is tough work. Because the larvae are most frequent in swift, broken water, weighted flies, split shot on the leader, and high density fly lines are usually necessary to put the imitation at the trout's level. Such outfits are just plain hard to cast and manipulate, but they frequently account for big trout. To provide some relief, I use a lead-tip line based on the lead shooting head of steelheading. Experimentation has shown that four to six feet of thirty-six-pound-test lead core will get the flies down quickly and can be handled with normal casting and fishing tactics. Scientific Anglers' new Hi-Speed Hi-D line is much more supple than lead core and a four- to six-foot piece of fifteen-weight makes an excellent lead tip. The lead tip is spliced to a running line, which has turned out to be the real key to this rig. This fluorescent orange line, made by Scientific Anglers, is about .029 inch in diameter and floats. High visibility makes following the line and detecting the strikes easy, while its small diameter and floatability cut down current drag and simplify mending.

In a stream, my favorite places to fish Wooly Worms are where the riffles dump into the head of a pool and in deep, broken-water runs. Cast the lead tip up and across, and as it comes downstream, lift your rod to keep a little tension. Mend if the currents begin to belly the running line. As the line passes your position, lower the rod and follow it. During the drift period, watch the line where it enters the water and be alert for the subtle tug of a take. When the line tightens in the currents below, permit it to swing across to your side. A strike at this time is usually savage. Strip in until only the head and five feet or so of running line remain in the water before making the next cast.

In lakes, use a sinking line and count it down. Work the fly slowly near the bottom with a strip/tease retrieve. Gather in a foot or so of line with a hand twist retrieve, pause for a few seconds, strip in a foot of line in one smooth motion, pause, and begin again with the hand twist. Fish usually take the fly softly so be constantly on the alert. For a good discussion on the use of sinking lines in lakes see Dan Blanton's article "Sinking Lines for Stillwater Trout" *(Fly Fisherman,* volume 10, number 6, 1979).

Adult megalopterans can also be significant. In *The Way of a Trout With a Fly,* G. E. M. Skues described his angling experiences with the alder, including 249 trout in sixteen days of fishing, over half these fish taken on this pattern. Skues fished his pattern wet in the manner of Charles Kingsley, whose *Chalk-Stream Studies* of 1858 established the alder as a recognized pattern. Their flies were tied with heron feathers, but a hair-wing fly or Poly-Caddis of correct shade is excellent. Normally these imitations are fished dry, but if the fish rise short or are otherwise reluctant to accept the pattern, fish it wet in the chalkstream tradition of Kingsley and Skues. Charles Wetzel, in his book *Trout Flies: Naturals and Imitations,* rates the Black Fishfly a killing pattern when fished wet. Fished wet or dry when the adults are about, a big hair-wing fishfly can be deadly. This imitation is tied in the same way as the large Hair-Wing Stonefly.

Keys to Dobsonflies, Fishflies, and Alderflies

Larvae

1a. Abdomen with seven pairs of lateral filaments and ending in one long terminal filament (fig. 8–8): family Sialidae, one genus *Sialis,* alderflies, twenty-three species. Lakes and streams, transcontinental.

1b. Abdomen with eight pairs of lateral filaments and without single, long terminal filament: family Corydalidae, found in East, Midwest, and Pacific Coast, absent from Rocky Mountain region . . . 2

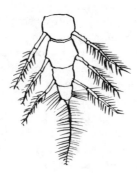

Fig. 8–8. Terminal end of abdomen of alderfly larva (Sialidae) showing single filament

2a. Each lateral filament of abdomen with a clump of bushlike gills at its base (fig. 8–4): genus *Corydalus*, dobsonflies (hellgrammites), two species. Riffles and stony runs in streams.

2b. Bushy gills absent: fishflies . . . 3

3a. East or Midwest . . . 4

3b. Pacific Coast . . . 6

4a. Respiratory tubes on ninth segment extended beyond tenth segment: genus *Chauliodes*, Tan Fishfly, two species. Lakes.

4b. Respiratory tubes short, not extending beyond tenth segment (fig. 8–9) . . . 5

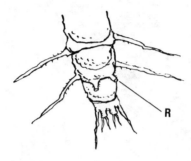

Fig. 8–9. Terminal end of abdomen of fishfly larva showing respiratory tubes (R)

5a. Top of head and thorax of uniform color: genus *Nigronia*, Black Fishfly, two species. Often found in riffles of trout streams.

5b. Top of head and thorax strongly patterned: genus *Neohermes*, five species. Streams (in debris or vegetation).

6a. Top of head and thorax distinctly patterned . . . 7

6b. Top of head and thorax of uniform color: genus *Dysmicohermes*, two (possibly three) species. Streams (in debris).

7a. Lateral filaments robust and longer than width of abdomen: genus *Neohermes* (see above)

7b. Lateral filaments delicate and about as long as abdomen is wide: genus *Protochauliodes*, five (possibly six) species. Streams (in debris).

Adults

1a. Wings with white spots or irregular white patches . . . 2

1b. Wings without white spots or patches . . . 3

2a. Very large, tan to grayish insects; males of eastern species with huge tusks; wings with numerous white spots: dobsonflies

2b. Insect black with irregular white bars across center of wings: Black Fishfly

3a. Insect uniformly gray-brown; wings slightly mottled; looks like a husky caddisfly; ten to fifteen millimeters long: alderflies

3b. Not as above: genera *Dysmicohermes*, *Neohermes*, and *Protochauliodes*. These must be separated on the basis of wing veins; see Merritt and Cummins (1978).

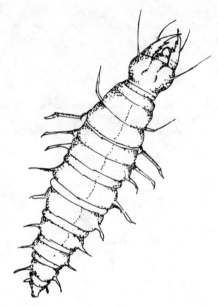

Fig. 8–10. Larva of Hydrophilidae beetle (aquatic)

BEETLES

The largest order of insects, Coleoptera, includes both terrestrial and aquatic forms of widely varying size, color, and shape. Beetles have a complete metamorphosis, and in the aquatic species both larvae and adults are eaten by trout. However, the larvae crawl from the water and erect pupation chambers in the stream's bank, and thus, the pupae are not available to the fish. Larvae of the predacious diving beetles (family Dytiscidae), whirligig beetles (family Gyrinidae), and the water scavenger beetles (family Hydrophilidae) are the most important to the angler. These strongly segmented larvae have well-developed legs and often external, filamentous gills (fig. 8–10). They range in color from olive to dirty yellow to browns and black, and in size from about ten to ninety millimeters long. These insects are found everywhere in the shallows of streams and lakes, particularly among the strands of aquatic vegetation and in debris where they crawl or swim in search of food. Larvae of the genus *Dytiscus* (family Dytiscidae) and a few others prefer riffles and stony runs in streams.

A Hair-Leg Wooly Worm fished deep among the vegetation in lakes or tumbled along the stream bottom is a fine representation of these larvae. Larvae of the predacious diving beetles can figure prominently as trout food.

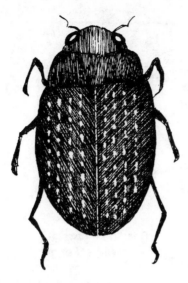

Fig. 8–11. Typical adult aquatic beetle

Adult aquatic beetles (fig. 8–11) vary from less than three to twenty millimeters. Most are dark brown to blackish and are found in the same general habitat as the larvae. Like the backswimmer and water boatman, these insects carry an air bubble against their bodies, and the pattern described for the water boatman is, thus, also an effective adult aquatic beetle imitation.

Terrestrial beetles become important when they stray onto the water, for trout readily seize these insects. Overhanging grass, shrubs, and trees are the most common avenues by which beetles get onto the water, and a good beetle imitation will often raise trout from areas overarched by plants.

While many beetles are the classic coffee bean shape, others are elongated and are strongly segmented between the thorax and abdomen. The name "Coleoptera" — formed by *coleo,* sheath, and *ptera,* wing — describes the thickened fore wings, or elytra, that cover the membranous hind wings of the resting adult. Marinaro clearly established that silhouette is the single most important characteristic of a good beetle pattern. Color can become significant if the trout are dimpling for a particular species. Such was the case during the years of heavy infestation of Japanese beetles.

The Crowe Beetle and Marinaro's Beetle held a special spot in my box of terrestrial imitations for many years. The mention of polypropylene yarn in *Selective Trout* started my experimentation with a host of poly patterns. One of the successful flies that emerged was the Poly-Beetle. It's built on the

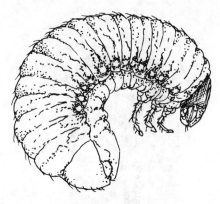

Fig. 8–12. Larva "grub" of june bug *(Phyllophaga)*

same concept as the Crowe Beetle. Lightweight and with a strong beetle silhouette, this fly has become a favorite. For general fishing, imitations in black or brown on #16 to #24 are most satisfactory.

The dimpling rise form to small beetles in the film is like the rise to ants and jassids. The rise is often falsely attributed to nymphing activity, and close scrutiny is usually necessary to ascertain the difference. A surface screen can greatly aid this interpretation. The classic V-form rise to terrestrial minutiae is most expertly described in Vince Marinaro's *A Modern Dry Fly Code.*

Of the larger beetles, the june bug *(Phyllophaga* spp.) is uniquely important to the fly fisher. Its larva is the thick, fleshy, white grub (fig. 8–12) that may become a serious pest in pastures, lawns, and cultivated fields where it voraciously feeds on roots, often destroying large patches of plants. The insects pupate in the soil and emerge during warm evenings in May and June to blunder in the night searching for a mate, frequently dropping onto the water with a resounding plop. Big browns hunting during the twilight of morning and evening and at night map sip the june bugs gently from the surface or splash at them greedily.

The hundred or so species of june bugs are dark rusty brown or black and average about twenty-five millimeters in length (fig. 8–13). The late Ben Egger of the Saint Paul Fly Tier's Club tied a pattern of trimmed deer hair overwound with a dark brown hackle. He rated this fly and the Giant Michigan Mayfly as the two patterns on which he had taken the most big browns at the surface.

Fish the June Bug on a floating line and use the heaviest tippet compatible with the conditions. If light tippets are necessary, check them frequently for fraying caused by casting this large fly. Plopping the artificial onto the water will improve the chances of attracting the attention of a large fish.

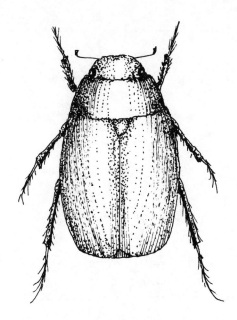

Fig. 8–13. Adult june bug *(Phyllophaga)*

Key to Beetles

This guide identifies the Coleoptera larvae, and includes notes on other stages.

1a. Legs with two claws each . . . 2
1b. Legs with one claw each . . . 3

2a. Abdomen ending in four conspicuous hooks (fig. 8–14); at least eight pairs of lateral filaments on the abdomen: family Gyrinidae, whirligig beetles. Adults occur in colonies on surface of ponds and slow waters of streams; they whirl about each other in an irregular fashion when disturbed; adults are shining black in color, nine to ten millimeters in length.

2b. Abdomen without terminal hooks; only six *or* fewer pairs lateral filaments on abdomen; abdomen tapering rearward (fig. 8–15): family Dytiscidae, predacious diving beetles. Most are pond and slow stream inhabitants, but members of genus *Dytiscus* prefer riffles; adults require aquatic vegetation and non-muddy bottom; second and third legs are widely separated; adult colors are shining black often marked with yellow, green, or rusty red; sizes range from one to forty millimeters.

3a. Abdomen ending in one or two tail-like filaments: family *Haliplidae,* crawling water beetles. Adults small, (two to five millimeters); live in algae mats and other vegetation in shallow water; yellow to brown mottled with black.

3b. Abdomen not ending in long filaments . . . 4

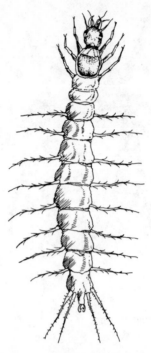

Fig. 8–14. Larva of whirligig beetle (Gyrinidae). Note four hooks at end of abdomen.

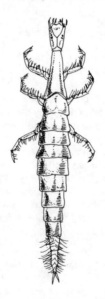

Fig. 8–15. Larva of predaceous diving beetle (Dytiscidae)

4a. Mandibles large and easily seen from above (fig. 8–16): family Hydrophilidae, water scavenger beetles. Adults have short clubbed antennae that are usually hidden under the head; occur in shallows of pools and lakes in vegetation; size ranges from one to forty millimeters; color is black, rarely yellow or brown.

4b. Mandibles inconspicuous from above; abdomen strongly segmented; segments very angular on upper side (fig. 8–17): family Elmidae, elmid beetles. Adults tiny (less than three and one-half millimeters); most occur in riffly areas of streams.

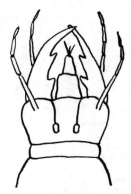

Fig. 8–16. Mandibles of water scavenger beetle (Hydrophilidae)

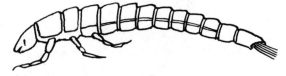

Fig. 8–17. Side view of elmid beetle larva (Elmidae)

MOTHS, BUTTERFLIES, AND SKIPPERS

In the extremely large insect order Lepidoptera (over eleven thousand species in North America) there are only a few truly aquatic species, which are all moths and are confined to the family Pyralididae. "Lepidoptera" (*lepido,* scales; *ptera,* wing) refers to the adult's scaly wings. The larvae of these insects are true aquatic caterpillars. They occur in a multitude of habitats: lakes, slow moving streams, hot springs, and intermittent streams. At least two species are known to inhabit rapidly moving water. These are in the genus *Parargyractis* and have about 120 unbranched gill filaments on the abdomen (fig. 8–18). They build silken canopies as large as twenty-five by one hundred millimeters over the surface of rocks. The insect moves

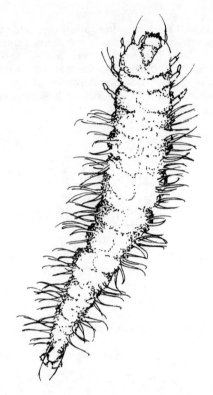

Fig. 8–18. Typical aquatic moth larva

about beneath this covering, feeding on algae that have grown on the rock. When mature, these straw-colored larvae are ten to twelve millimeters long. Several species of these larvae breathe air, but most have true aquatic respiration and are equipped with long, slender, filamentous gills. The fast water species pupate under a canopy of silk. When the adult is fully formed, it escapes and swims or floats to the surface. Mature larvae of the slow water species are twenty to twenty-five millimeters in length and yellow or whitish with a dark head.

Adults of the aquatic species are rather small; grey, brown, or blackish in color; and usually seen near the water on summer evenings. Eggs are generally deposited on vegetation although in the western species *Parargyractis truckeealis,* the female crawls beneath the surface and lays eggs directly on the underside of rocks.

A highly successful night pattern with a silhouette strongly resembling a moth was recently developed by my colleague Ed Osypowski. During the first month of its evolution, this fly produced three trout over twenty inches for him and earned its name, the Polish Warbonnet. The fly is tied of natural deer body hair on hooks #2 to #8. The tail is a clump of hair tied short, the body is trimmed hair (shaped like the June Bug), the wing is a large clump of hair tied over the back, and the head is formed by the butt ends of the wing. The fly is heavily dressed with paste floatant and twitched, then rested, on the surface. Regardless of whether the fish take this pattern as a moth, stonefly, caddis, mouse, or other food organism, its effectiveness has earned it a permanent niche in my fly boxes.

The caterpillars (larvae) of terrestrial Lepidoptera occasionally fall onto the water, especially the loopers or inchworms (family Geometridae). The loopers are smooth, bright green to browns, and ten to fifteen millimeters long (fig. 8–19). They feed on leaves, and when mature descend to the ground on silken threads and there pupate. Those accidently descending to the water often drag on the surface for some time before the silk breaks. Trout feed readily, often greedily, on these larvae. Imitations are fashioned of trimmed, deer-body hair on #10 to #14, 3XL. This pattern is fished dead drift or dragging lightly downstream on the surface.

Fig. 8–19. Measuring worm (larva of Geometridae)

Don't underrate the inchworms. They are widespread and the second largest family of lepidopterans (over twelve hundred species in North America). They don't form a season-long supply of food for the trout, but rather are abundant for a few weeks in late spring and early summer. During that time they excite even the biggest browns to feed recklessly at the surface. In the Midwest they appear with the Brown Drakes and wane during the Giant Michigan Mayfly hatch. It's a euphoric time: the angler can take big trout on inchworms during the day and on big Drakes at night.

9

The Ant and the Grasshopper

Terrestrials — the word has come to suggest meandering streams in pastoral settings. On such a stream the importance of land-bred insects as trout food was first clearly documented. Surrounding Carlisle, Pennsylvania, is an area of limestone valleys rich in colonial and Civil War heritage, where flow the meadow streams the Letort, Yellow Breeches, Big Spring, Green Spring, Cedar Run, Falling Springs, and others. They have been a wellspring of information on the trout and his feeding habits, but none is so revealing as that on terrestrials.

The significance of these insects in the trout's diet was established by Vince Marinaro, and his patterns and ideas have been the prototypes of all the following works on terrestrials. His lucid observations and careful arguments are eloquently set forth in *A Modern Dry Fly Code.* At the moment of discovery, Marinaro was lying on the bank of the Letort watching a small trout feed when he happened to notice minute insects floating in the film. He quickly got a cheesecloth sieve and found, to his delight, a whole assortment of tiny land creatures in the surface drift. There were jassids, beetles, and several sizes and colors of ants. Grasshoppers and other land organisms were later found on the surface. With such a rich terrestrial menagerie constantly overhead, the trout naturally become extremely surface conscious. On many streams, they rise freely throughout the day, the soft dimpling rises belying the stature of the feeding fish. Anglers who have

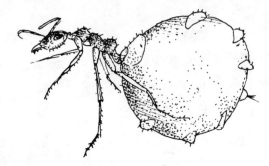

Fig. 9–1. Honey ant replete

not fished with terrestrials have missed an exciting and productive part of fly fishing. For further study I would recommend Marinaro's text and Gerald Almy's recent book, *Tying and Fishing the Terrestrials.* It's a fine study devoted entirely to this aspect of fly fishing.

ANTS

Included in the order Hymenoptera *(hymeno,* membrane; *ptera,* wing; referring to the four membranous wings) are ants, bees, wasps, and others. Within this vast order of insects, the ants (family Formicidae) are of special interest to the angler. They are the most numerous of all terrestrial animals and occur in abundance in every land ecosystem except the polar regions. Their life styles range from that of the large, wood boring carpenter ants to mound builders; from fierce, predacious warriors to ants that keep aphid cows and honey ants that store their winter's food supply of honeydew in the bodies of specialized workers called repletes (fig. 9–1).

Ants vary in size from about one millimeter to as much as thirteen (more in some tropical species). Their structure is unique; the first one or two segments of the abdomen are sharply pinched into a slender waist (the pedicel), and the remainder of the abdomen (gaster) is greatly enlarged. Their bodies are commonly clothed with minute hairs. The stout legs are a prominent feature of the Formicidae.

Like bees and many wasps, ants are social insects, living in colonies. Maintenance of the colony is divided among three distinct castes: workers, females, and males. Workers (fig. 9–2) are wingless and form the vast majority of individuals within any colony. This group enlarges and repairs the nest, cares for the queen and young, secures food, and defends the community. During the foraging season, workers bustle about in the foliage

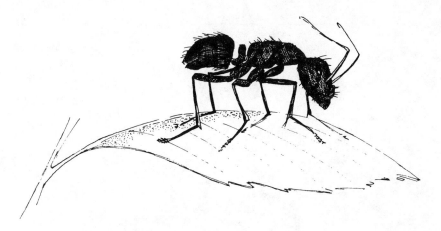

Fig. 9–2. Worker ant

and on the ground in search of food and are often blown or fall upon the water. All during the warm seasons, ants can be seen floating in trout streams. Each colony has one reproducing female, the queen, which may be distinguished by her large size and enormous gaster. Queens mate only once, but lay eggs continuously in the warm months. They live thirteen to fifteen years. Males are intermediate in size between workers and the queen, and are winged.

Periodically, several virgin queens and numerous males are produced. These sexually mature ants leave the nest in a great swarm to perform their nuptial flight. In the northern temperate zone these flights often occur in June, or July at high elevations, although I have encountered them throughout the warm seasons. After the female mates, she bites off her wings and founds a new colony. The winged males or drones (fig. 9–3) die shortly after swarming. If the flight occurs near a stream or lake these flying ants may literally carpet the water's surface, stimulating feeding orgies among the trout. The insects may hold their wings upright or the wings may be in the film. Patterns should imitate the natural's wing position.

If ever there was a gourmet's pièce de résistance for the trout, it's the ant. Trout often ignore a good hatch of aquatic insects to feed on drifting ants. Ed Hewitt tasted ants and concluded the reason was their flavor. It's academic whether the pungent formic acid flavor of these insects or some other factor makes them so attractive to the fish. Fact is they are, and a selection of ant imitations is essential to any well-stocked fly box.

The flies should stress the swollen gaster and narrowed pedicel of the natural in order to achieve the correct silhouette (fig. 9–4). They must also

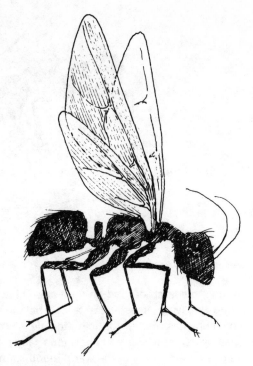

Fig. 9–3. Winged male ant or drone

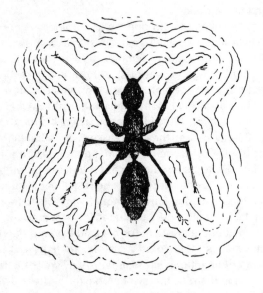

Fig. 9–4. The pattern formed by an ant in the surface film is very characteristic

lie *down in the film* rather than sit up high on the surface. Marinaro clarifies the reason: "I could not understand immediately why I had never detected the presence of the large ants in my previous examinations and I returned to the stream again to discover the reason for this defection. After a careful inspection, I found to my surprise that the large ants did not float on the surface of the water but drifted awash, partly submerged and flush with the surface, wings sodden and blending with the background in such a way as to make them completely invisible to the angler." My Para-Ant's effectiveness, I believe, is due to the way it rides in the water: low, partially submerged, and flush with the film.

Ants can also be fished wet. When the floating insects are swept into broken water they are submerged and become a component of subsurface drift. Hard-bodied flies (made of thread or another material) are best for wet fly angling because they sink readily. Bob McCafferty tied such flies and fished them with devastating success on Pennsylvania's spring creeks. He would cast across to likely holding lies and allow the current to slowly draw the fly away. It's a trick that has proved itself many times.

Wasps and bees are not infrequently a component of surface drift. For these insects a large, Spent Ant pattern is quite effective.

Charles Cotton's advice to "fish fine and far off" reaches across the centuries to the angler who wants to fish ants and other terrestrial minutiae. Low, clear waters and highly selective, leader-shy trout make ultrafine tackle a minimum requisite for such fishing. Each trout must be carefully stalked and observed from several angles before the fisher eases into position to make the presentation. If the capricious wind cooperates and the pattern is right, the angler may suddenly find himself attached to a surprisingly large fish by a frail leader. If all goes well the fish is finally captured, photographed, and released to provide sport another day. It's all a marvelous and unparalleled experience.

GRASSHOPPERS AND CRICKETS

In those lazy, hazy, dog days of late summer, while the ants busily lay in a winter store, the grasshoppers fiddle their time away, leaping about in wild abandon and often plopping carelessly into trout streams. If the ant is a gourmet treat for trout, then the grasshopper is a glutton's delight. Grasshoppers (fig. 9–5) are strong swimmers and strike for shore with powerful kicks. Even the very largest trout are aroused by this activity and will feed readily. There's no mistaking the sucking splash of a trout that's eating hoppers.

These are principally meadow and field insects, and in the halcyon days of August, when the warm winds rustle the tansies and goldenrod, hopper

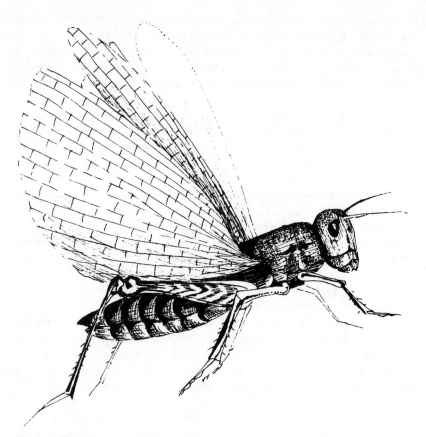

Fig. 9–5. Grasshopper in flight

fishing is at its pinnacle. Rises will not be as frequent as during a hatch, and the angler must often anticipate the trout, plopping the fly onto the water to be fished dead drift at the edge of overhanging grass and shrubs. The plop of the fly is usually sufficient to signal its presence to the trout. Twitching the big imitation will often raise a reluctant fish, but care must be exercised to avoid causing unnecessary disturbance with the leader, as this may put the fish down. When a rising fish is found, it should be stalked carefully from shore if at all possible, and the fly should be presented on a curve cast to a point several feet above the rise, as the fish often drift back to take the hopper then return upstream to the feeding station. The low, clear waters at this time of the year require a fine tippet, but casting these large flies will quickly fray it. Therefore, if a fine leader point must be used, check it frequently, as large fish are often engaged during this period.

Ernie Schwiebert's Letort Hopper was the first fly to effectively imitate the low-slung silhouette of these big insects. It was baptized in the Letort and proved its worth by consistently taking that stream's superselective trout. Dave's Hopper, developed by the gifted fly tier and angler Dave Whitlock, earned its laurels on the big trout of the upper Madison in Yellowstone Park. I prefer the simplicity of the Letort Hopper, but the wing style of Dave's Hopper. This composite fly has a most appealing appearance and a simple design: a salute to the genius of Schwiebert and Whitlock.

Orthopterans have a gradual metamorphosis: egg to true nymph to adult. The true nymph looks like a miniature version of the adult, but lacks fully developed wings. Imitations of the immature insect can be successful in early summer. These should be dressed on hooks of appropriate size and with short wings to most realistically suggest the nymph. As the season progresses, increase the size of the imitations to match the maturing insects.

Another Orthopteran, the cricket, is prime trout food, too (fig. 9–6). Ed Shenk's Letort Cricket is responsible for the Pennsylvania record brown trout taken on a dry fly: a nine-pounder caught by Ed Koch in the Letort during August 1962.

In lakes, the trick is to let them lie on the surface until you can't stand it any longer — and that's still not long enough. Fish move about in lakes searching for food, and you have to give them a chance to find the fly.

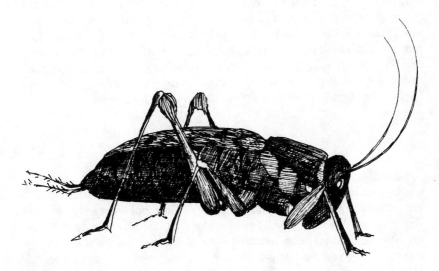

Fig. 9–6. A field cricket

10

The Non-insects

Crustaceans, food fishes, and the other organisms in this chapter are what some fly fishers call miscellaneous food items. Because they're the non-insects, it is sometimes convenient to lump them together, but the unfortunate result has been an overlooking of their distribution and importance. Minnow imitations probably account for more big trout each year than any other imitations, and crustaceans are an integral part of the life of a trout. The other organisms are either of local consequence or highly significant at special times. A mouse imitation can produce some exciting night fishing, and big trout have fallen to imitations of worms, leeches, tadpoles, and others.

CRUSTACEANS

Trout become familiar with the crustaceans very early in life. The abundant, minute Daphnia or water flea (order Cladocera, fig. 10–1) occurs in all waters, and comprises as much as ninety-five percent and rarely less than ten percent of the fish fry diet. In some lakes, especially bog lakes and lakes at higher elevations (where insects are not abundant), Daphnia form a large, if not the main, component of the diet of trout of *all* age categories. These .2- to 3-millimeter-long crustaceans graze on plankton (algae and protozoans) and minute particles of detritus. Where other food organisms are abundant,

Fig. 10–1. Typical water flea (Daphnia)

the growing trout abandon the Daphnia in search of larger foods, and other crustaceans become important, mainly scuds, cressbugs, and crayfish. These three organisms are sometimes overlooked by the fly fisher, but they are widespread and numerous, and in many water systems are the principle foods of the trout.

The class Crustacea (from *crustaceus,* having a hard shell) is part of the phylum Arthropoda (joined legs).

In addition to the following orders, there are a number of other crustaceans found in fresh waters. These are the fairy shrimp (order Anostraca), tadpole shrimp (order Notostraca), clam shrimp (order Conchostraca), seed shrimp (order Podacopa), copepods (order Eucopepoda), fish lice (order Branchiura), oppossum shrimp (order Nypidacea), and freshwater shrimp (order Decapoda). These organisms are either very small, on the bottom of extremely deep lakes, or so restricted in habitat that imitations are essentially useless. Most anglers will never encounter them.

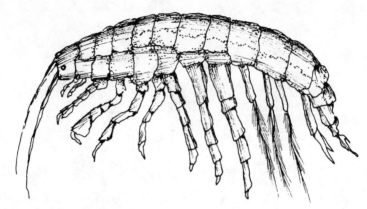

Fig. 10–2. Typical scud (Amphipoda)

Scuds

There are about fifty species of scuds varying in length from five to twenty millimeters and in color from reds and purples to tans, grays, and olives. Their body plan is distinctive (fig. 10–2). Like other crustaceans, the head and first thoracic segment are fused into a cephalothorax. There are seven more free segments in the thorax, six segments in the abdomen, and a terminal segment, the telson. The body is flattened at the sides and hinged like an armadillo. There are seven pairs of legs, one pair on each thoracic segment. The first two pairs are club-shaped gnathopods ("jaw feet"), which hold food items. The others are unspecialized, hence, the order "Amphipoda" *(amphi,* both; *poda,* legs). There is a pair of appendages on each of the six abdominal segments. The first three are bushy and propel the scud when it swims. Active, agile swimmers, they dart about the bottom or among the vegetation in search of food. During swimming the thoracic legs are pointed to the rear and the body is held straight. For this reason, scud patterns should not be tied humpbacked, but with a straight body.

The breeding period is governed by water temperature and generally occurs during the warm months. Many species breed only once during their one-year or shorter life cycle; a few produce multiple broods. The females carry their fertilized eggs in a special abdominal cavity called a marsupium which protects the developing eggs. The young hatch in the marsupium and are released when the female molts.

Scuds occur in all types of streams and lakes, from temporary to permanent, from swamps to springs, from acid to alkaline, from large to small, but like trout, they require water with a high oxygen level. Oddly, all but a couple of species are never found deeper than three feet *(Hyallela azteca* is common in deeper water, *Pontoporeia affinis* is found as deep as one thousand feet in Lake Superior).

The three species most frequently encountered in trout waters are *Gammarus limnaeus, Hyallela azteca,* and *Crangonyx gracilis.* They can be startlingly abundant. Robert Pennak reports, in *Fresh Water Invertebrates of the United States,* sampling populations that exceeded ten thousand per square meter in the rooted plants of spring creeks. Little wonder they're fed upon by trout.

Like most crustaceans, scuds feed and move most actively during the night and on overcast days. Species of *Gammarus* are a principle component of nocturnal behavioral drift. Thus, the best hours for fishing imitations are dusk through dawn. On overcast days scuds are mildly active at midday. On bright days they hole up in vegetation or in bottom debris. In streams, fish scud imitations along the bottom, either dead drift on a long tippet or with a start and stop twitching retrieve. In lakes, the fly is twitched along slowly just above submersed weeds.

Trout will actively root scuds out of weed beds. Charlie Fox has reported that in Pennsylvania's spring creeks the fish begin rooting in early winter. They thrust their bodies into the plants, wiggle violently, then back out and intercept any dislodged scuds or cressbugs. Such behavior shows the importance of these crustaceans in the winter diet of trout and the obvious familiarity of fish with this fare.

Cressbugs

The body of these crustaceans is flattened top and bottom and looks like an elongated, jointed disk (fig. 10–3). They are of the order Isopoda *(iso,*

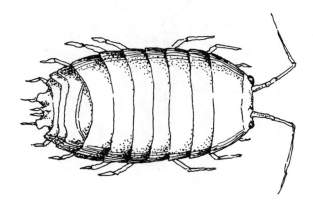

Fig. 10–3. Typical cressbug (Isopoda)

equal; *poda,* legs; referring to the sameness of all the legs). The fifty or so species in North American waters range in length from five to twenty millimeters and their color varies. Those from the limestone springs near Carlisle, Pennsylvania, are a dark straw color; others are medium to dark gray, reddish, or blackish. Populations occur mostly in spring creeks and cool, unpolluted lake edges. In such places they can be extremely abundant. Like the scud, this organism is a scavanger found on or near aquatic vegetation, especially watercress, where it crawls in search of food. When dislodged, cressbugs simply drift with the current until they contact vegetation or the bottom. Imitations are fished dead drift on a long tippet.

Crayfish

These crustaceans are found in all types of aquatic environments where the concentration of calcium exceeds three parts per million; there are even species that colonize wet meadows. They are well distributed throughout the United States, being absent only in a few areas of the Rocky Mountains. These crustaceans (fig. 10–4) provide a large, juicy morsel for trout and

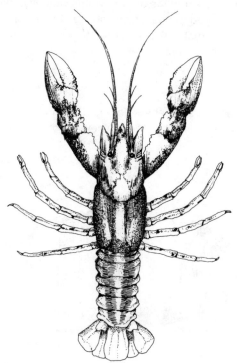

Fig. 10–4. Female crayfish (Decapoda)

other gamefish, and "soft shells" are a favored bait of many fishermen. Crayfish belong to the order Decapoda *(deca,* ten; *poda,* legs; from their ten walking legs).

Research has shown that given a choice, fish select the smallest crayfish first and prefer females to males. The females have smaller chelipeds ("pinchers") than the males and are less aggressive, fleeing at the approach of a predator. The male stands and fights. These anatomical and behavioral differences account for the fish's selection of females over males.

I keep my pattern small, and proportion it like the female. The fly is weighted slightly and tied upside down to reduce snagging. It is also reversed on the hook since the startled natural swims backward with a chopping motion of its tail. The color of individual specimens varies markedly from location to location even within the same watershed since pigmentation can change somewhat to match the background colors of the habitat. However, most crayfish are a brownish orange to olive brown. Artificials tied in these colors will mimic the naturals of nearly all waters.

Like the scuds and cressbugs, these crustaceans are nocturnal, scavenging in the darkness for food. Their restriction to the bottom necessitates weighted flies and sinking lines except in shallow water. At night, fish the gravel bars and shallow, rocky runs where trout forage for minnows and crayfish, working your fly close to the bottom with a jerky retrieve that apes the retreating female.

FOOD FISHES

Trout devour small fish of many species, including their own fry, but the most important food fishes are the minnows, sculpins, and sticklebacks. The minnow family (Cyprinidae) is the largest fish family containing over fifteen hundred species worldwide. It includes daces (fig. 10–5), chubs, shiners, and carp. Species of minnows are widely distributed in streams and lakes of the world and are generally only a few inches in length. There are some exceptions: the fall fish, largest minnow native to the eastern United States, may reach eighteen inches in length; the Colorado squawfish, largest of all American minnows, has a maximum length of five feet. Carp reach a length of several feet and may weigh in excess of twenty pounds.

Numerous patterns employing feather or hair wings have been developed to imitate the minnows. The Gray Ghost, Blacknose Dace, Mickey Finn, Mylar Minnow, various Maribou Streamers, and the Matuka have been the most successful imitations for me. Many of the important minnows of our streams and lakes are described in Keith Fulsher's book *Tying and Fishing the Thunder Creek Series.* His recognition that color and form are important in minnow imitations is a big step forward in this area of fly fishing. As

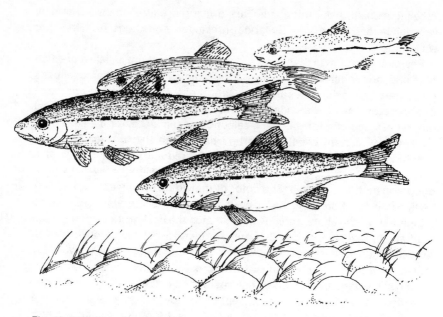

Fig. 10–5. The blacknose dace

knowledge of minnow habits and coloration expands, fishing these imitations is certain to become even more effective. For very large minnow representations, the Blonde series developed by Joe Brooks is most satisfactory. Tied on up-eyed salmon hooks in #2 through #3/0, this fly is effective for big trout.

The Cottidae family, or sculpins, are recognized by their large, flattened heads, widely spread pectoral fins, and smooth skins (fig. 10–6). This family is largely marine, being represented in fresh water mainly by the genus *Cottus.* These fish are dispersed over North America and are generally grayish to olive brown, mottled with patches of dark brown or black. Sculpins prowl the labyrinths of the bottom rubble in search of food, camouflaged by their mottled coloration. They are a favored food of the trout, and on western streams are widely collected for bait. Western fly fishermen are never without a variety of imitations of this important food fish. Dave Whitlock's Sculpin as shown in Art Flick's *Master Fly Tying Guide* and Don Gapen's Muddler Minnow are excellent, time-tested patterns.

Sticklebacks (family Gasterosteidae) are interesting little fish found in streams and along the shores of lakes (fig. 10–7). Their range is essentially the same as the trout's. They can erect and lock in place the spines in the dorsal fin. In the spring they build a nest in aquatic vegetation. The male secretes a glue from his vent and swims around the leaves of aquatic plants, pulling them together and fastening them to form a nest not unlike that of an oriole. After the female is wooed and won and eggs are laid, the male zealously guards the nest. Trout foraging among the weed beds will seize the sticklebacks. A thinly dressed muddler is a fine imitation.

There are several excellent tactics for fishing the long flies. The standard approach is to cast across or across and down with a floating line and work the fly with the rod as the current swings it back across to your side. This retrieve usually elicits a hard strike from the trout, not infrequently resulting in a broken tippet if the angler is unprepared. Use a stout tippet, 3X

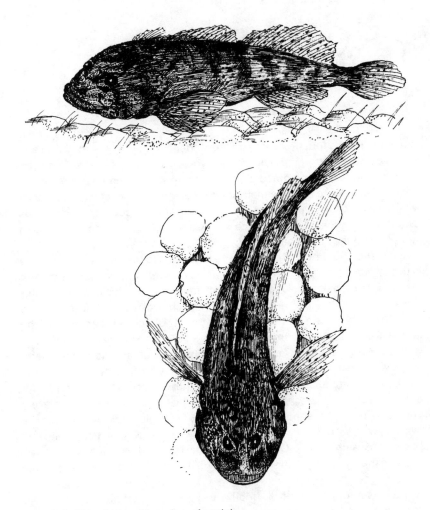

Fig. 10–6. Side view and top view of sculpin

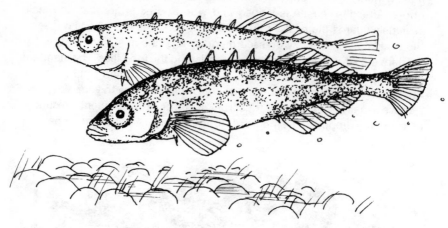

Fig. 10–7. Sticklebacks

minimum. Hold a foot or so of extra line under a finger of your rod hand and let it slide out through the guides when you pull the hook home. This extra line will absorb the combined shock of the trout's hit and your instinctive, hard strike. I like to use this method in riffles and rapids, casting so the fly will swing across just upstream of a rock, log, or deep pocket. If the water is over three feet deep, a sinking line will be a big help in getting the fly down and working it at the trout's level.

Spin fishermen know that one of the best ways to take trout on hardware is to cast upstream and reel the lure back along the bottom just faster than the current. It's also a deadly way to fish streamers. For this method I prefer a floating or sinking tip line so I can see it and control the slack. The leader is eight to ten feet long with a three-foot tippet. Clinch the streamer to the leader and then pinch a microshot right above the knot — in extra heavy water, a BB-sized shot. Cast the fly straight up or up and across and let it drift a ways so it can sink, then begin the retrieve. Strip in the slack line and keep the fly coming down just fast enough that it isn't drifting (barely faster than the current). Twitch the rod tip so the fly jumps off the bottom every couple of feet. The shot will cause the fly to angle back down after the twitch. Try to work the fly down next to rocks, drop-offs, fast currents, and so on, and watch closely. Often you'll feel the take as the trout noses out and sucks in the jigging fly. Other times though, the only signal is a twitch on the line.

The Leisenring lift, a most effective way to take trout on streamers, is a combination of these two tactics. The fly is cast up and across and jigged down current. As the fly passes the angler, he follows the line with the rod and then works the fly back, as in the down and across approach. When the line tightens in the downstream currents, the fly abruptly changes direction, begins rising toward the surface, and speeds up. Such apparent escape movement is sure to trigger the predatory instincts of any nearby trout. If you can place the fly so that it jumps off the bottom right where you suspect a trout is holding (around rocks, near logs), it will increase the chances of a tackle-shattering take.

Fig. 10–8. A boulder-strewn run on Spring Creek in Pennsylvania

Joe Brooks, a master with the long flies, originated the Blonde series for salt water, but later adapted them successfully to rivers like the Snake, the Madison, and the Yellowstone. He had seen a trout take a minnow from the side, turn it, and swallow it head first and reasoned that a trout would be more apt to take a streamer if it was presented sideways. Always a creative angler, he coupled his saltwater flies with the greased line tactic used by Atlantic salmon fishermen and developed a most successful streamer tactic, the broadside float. The idea is to *drift* the fly sideways in the current. If the flow is uniform from bank to bank, the angler only has to cast across the stream and follow the line down with the rod. The fly will drift along sideways in the current. Most trout streams do not flow uniformly from bank to bank; there's a strong tongue of current in the center or to one side. Drifting the fly in currents requires that the line be mended as often as necessary to prevent the fly from swinging down and across. If the current is strongest in the center and the angler wishes to fish its far side, he should drop the line across and slightly upstream with an S-cast (jiggle the rod tip as the line straightens so it will fall in a series of S-shaped bends). The swift water between the fly and the angler will soon cause the line to bow downstream ahead of the fly. At this point the angler must lift this downstream bow and flop it back upstream; otherwise, the fly will accelerate down and across. When the fly is cast into the fast current, it will move downstream faster than the line. In this case the bow develops upstream and the line must be mended *downstream.* The mends keep the line moving at the same rate as the fly and thus eliminate drag. If you haven't used this drifting, broadside float, by all means practice until you've mastered it. It is a most valuable streamer tactic.

As minnows foraging on drifting insects or scuds after dark are an easy mark for the trout, night fishing with streamers can be very productive. I have had the greatest success with black Muddlers. The trick is to fish them slowly. This is where the broadside float is handy. Trout often back down into the tail of a pool to forage at dusk, and if the fly comes down slow and easy, they seem more prone to accept it than if it's zipping along. The take is often soft; a mere tightening sensation of the line may be the only clue that a fish has picked up the drifting fly. There's that instant, as you pull the hook home, when you're not sure if the trout is five inches or five pounds.

Trout in lakes take streamers readily. There's no current, but the fish can still be choosy. The secret to working a streamer in lakes is to try different retrieves at different depths. A jigging retrieve near the bottom can be extremely productive one time and fail dismally the next. Sometimes the fly must be fished right at the surface. Once I encountered trout splashing at the surface and was sure they were taking the midges that were hatching.

The tiny pupal imitation went unnoticed. Then as I stood there, frustrated, I saw a minnow wiggle up and take a midge. He quickly disappeared down the gullet of a fine rainbow. A Muddler Minnow, with its buoyant deer hair head, was the answer, but it had to be fished correctly: twitch, twitch, then rest for five to ten seconds, then twitch, twitch. Trout — often the biggest — also pick off minnows feeding on hatching insects in streams. This is especially noticeable when small insects are hatching; the trout can get a bigger mouthful from the minnow than from the small invertebrates. It pays to watch and see what is actually happening rather than make inaccurate assumptions.

Since these long flies are wind-resistant and heavy, I prefer a rod with sufficient power to drive them without working me too hard. For the run-of-the-mill sizes (6 through 12) a six-weight rod is just the ticket, but for the big Blondes and other oversized streamers, a number eight casts the fly much easier.

Streamers certainly should be a part of every angler's big trout tactics.

FROGS AND TOADS

The class Amphibia (*amphi*, both; *bia*, life) received its name because the young live in water and have gills, and the adults live on land and have lungs. Tadpoles (immature frogs and toads) are very abundant in streams, ponds, and lakes during the spring. They hug the edges and weed beds, venturing into deep water only when disturbed. Brook trout in the "lake" areas of Wisconsin's Bois Brule River are often seen searching the openings in weed beds for tadpoles and sticklebacks. A tiny, black Muddler is effective on these fish.

Small lakes and ponds are often nearly overrun with tadpoles. In the morning and evening hours, trout cruise the shorelines, and you can be sure that they feed heavily on these young amphibians. The English are highly advanced stillwater anglers, and John Goddard is acclaimed as one of the best. His Tadpolly fly has been very productive wherever he has fished it: "In fact so readily has it been accepted on many waters I am inclined to think that trout may feed on the natural far more often than is generally supposed, and this could well account for the success of the common and widely used black type of lure." Fish the fly with a medium fast twitching retrieve.

It's well known that big browns and other big trout will take all kinds of the larger aquatic food organisms. Adult frogs are no exception. Where they occur in abundance, they will be significant, and frog-colored bass poppers or hair bugs can produce some excellent night fishing.

MICE, RATS, AND SHREWS

These members of the class Mammalia *(mamma,* milk gland) are widely distributed and occur in woodland and meadow areas, often in the vicinity of streams. The deermouse *(Peromyscus* spp., fig. 10–9) and the meadow vole *(Microtus* spp.) are the most widespread and common mice. As they rummage in grasses or brush near a stream they occasionally fall into the water. Additionally, they take to the water as a matter of course when active at night, swimming across streams or prowling along the edges.

Shrews are the smallest mammals. They are highly active predators that voraciously consume insects, worms, and other small animals. The northern water shrew *(Sorex palustris),* which is distributed across the northern United States, is adapted for an aquatic existence. The hind feet are enlarged, paddlelike, and covered with stiff hairs. The middle toes are partially webbed. These creatures may actually race along the surface for short distances. They dive to the bottom in shallow water and swim very rapidly when foraging.

An imitation of a mouse or shrew is considered by many anglers to be the night lure par excellence for big trout, especially browns. My good friend Royce Dam ties his mouse patterns with caribou hair so they ride partially submerged like the natural. The fly is cast onto the bank, or very close to it, carefully pulled into the water, and retrieved with a slow twitching action. A twelve- to fifteen-pound test tippet is necessary to cast the fly and handle the big fish so often encountered.

Fig. 10–9. Whitefooted deermouse *(Peromyscus)*

LAMPREYS

Lampreys are eel-like animals that live in both marine and freshwater environments. They are not true eels since they lack jaws (hence, they are of the class Agnatha, "without jaws"). These animals have gained notoriety among anglers because several species are fish parasites. Not all members of this family (Petromyzontidae), however, deserve the blood-thirsty reputation. The brook lampreys, of which there are a number of species, are a common nonparasitic form.

Lampreys inhabit all types of water systems but spawn in the gravel beds of streams in spring. The young (ammocetes) drift downstream until they find a mud bank or silt bed. They burrow in the soft bottom and live there several years, feeding on algae and other bottom materials. When they attain adult size, the ammocetes metamorphose to the adult and gain the disk-shaped, sucker mouth for which they are so well known. Adults vary from a few inches in length for the brook lamprey to a couple of feet for the sea lamprey. Transformation occurs in the fall and the parasitic forms begin to feed on the blood and body juices of fishes. The nonparasitic forms do not feed; they just dwell in the river until the spawning season. After spawning both forms die.

When spawning occurs, the streams may be full of these wiggling, snakelike animals. The larger, parasitic forms are not generally preyed upon by fish, but the smaller brook lampreys are a good meal for the trout. When these creatures are making their spawning run, fish a four- to six-inch long, tan strip fly in places known to hold big trout.

WORMS

Bob Pelzl is a knowledgeable fly fisher from Albuquerque, New Mexico, but his descriptions of fishing the San Juan River seemed like wild exaggerations, even for a fisherman. The photographs he showed me quelled my doubts, and when he invited me to fish the river with him, I accepted with excitement. "We'll use worms," Bob said. "They're really hot up in the quality water." Before I could speak, he pulled several flies from his nymph box and dropped them into my hand. "These were developed by Jim Aubrey as a scud imitation. When he tried them on the San Juan they proved incredibly effective. It wasn't until later that we found the worms and realized Jim's fly was a shrimp turned worm."

The worms we collected proved to be truly aquatic earthworms of the family Lumbriculidae. These members of the phylum Annelida get their name from *anulus* (ring), referring to the segmented body. They live in the bottom sands and silts of many rivers and sometimes, like in the San Juan, become extremely abundant. The ones we found were about forty millimeters long. Bob explained that at certain times of the year the normally reddish worms are yellow in color. This may be linked to the reproductive cycle.

I later met Jim Aubrey and have since shared several delightful fishing trips with him and Bob Pelzl. "The shrimp was originally tied as a cutthroat fly," Jim explained. He later proved his point by taking several fine cutthroats from the Yellowstone River on the fly. Jim refuses to call his pattern a worm and lightheartedly takes the brunt of many worm jokes. Shrimp or worm, it's an effective fly.

LEECHES

Leeches or bloodsuckers (class Hirudinae, fig. 10–10) are frequent inhabitants of marshes, ponds, lakes, and the slow water areas of streams. Of the five hundred worldwide species, about forty-five occur in the United States. These are placed in four families. The Glossiphoniidae and Piscicolidae lack jaws and have clear blood. The former are carnivores that eat snails and other small invertebrates while the latter are fish and turtle parasites. Leeches in the family Erpobdellidae lack jaws but have red blood.

Fig. 10–10. Typical leech (Hirudinae)

They are mostly carnivores, and only occasionally parasites on frogs and fish. The Hirudidae have red blood also, and in addition have true jaws which may be toothed. This family constitutes the bloodsuckers that readily attack warm-blooded animals.

The body of a leech is elongated, flattened top and bottom, and tapered at the ends. It is divided into thirty-four true segments each of which is subdivided into several superficial segments. Sucker disks occur at each end of the body; the posterior disk is the larger and is used to hold the leech firmly to plants, rocks, debris, or a host organism. The anterior disk is used during feeding. Paired eyes at the head aid in hunting.

Leeches are every color of the artist's palette. As a rule they are spotted, mottled, streaked, or striped, often in reds, oranges, and yellows. The background color is usually gray, brownish, olive, or black. Some are nearly translucent.

Sizes range from 5 millimeters to as much as 450 millimeters while swimming; leeches are usually much shorter at rest than when swimming. The red-blooded leeches are excellent swimmers, their bodies undulating fluidly. The clear-blooded leeches are nonswimmers and curl up when disturbed.

Breeding occurs in the spring after the leech has eaten. Eggs are laid in a cocoon from May to as late as November. The adult overwinters, buried in the bottom well below the frost line. Leeches may live for five years or more.

Leeches prefer shallow, quiet water. Because they cling to objects, they are rare where the bottom is pure mud or clay. They are especially prevalent across the northern part of the Midwest and in the eastern and western mountain states. They may become extremely abundant; as many as seven hundred per square meter have been reported in some northern lakes.

Most trout anglers know what leeches are, but few have attached much significance to them as trout food. However, they are definitely important. The success of the black maribou streamer is due in large part to the fact that it is an excellent leech imitation. For my leech pattern, I use a strip fly tied Matuka-style. The strip fly concept was shown to me by Royce Dam, custom fly tier and highly experienced angler from Franklin, Wisconsin. It produces the most realistic imitation of leeches. Worked slowly with a pulsing retrieve, the Strip Leech is so effective that it has become my favorite fly when prospecting for big trout.

SNAILS AND CLAMS

The Latin word *molluscus,* a soft, thin shelled nut, is the root of the name of the phylum to which snails and clams belong — the Mollusca.

Contrary to what one might think, freshwater snails (class Gastropoda) are a common food item for trout. In fact, there's a variety of brown trout, known as the gillaroo, that occurs in some Irish lakes and exists on a steady diet of snails and clams. Its stomach walls are thick to guard against the abrasive shells.

These organisms inhabit nearly every type of freshwater system and are sometimes present in numbers beyond imagination. They are especially prevalent on submerged vegetation in lakes and spring creeks. Snail flies have not been very popular with fly fishers, but imitations can be effective. Charlie Brooks discusses a pattern in his book *The Trout and the Stream* and says, "In areas where snails form a portion of the trout's diet, it works very well. Whether the fish take it for a snail, I know not."

In his book *The Super Flies of Still Water,* John Goddard states that snails in English reservoirs occasionally float at the surface during July and August and cause heavy feeding by the trout. The fish become highly selective during such periods, then as Goddard points out " . . . on those rare occasions when it (a snail fly) is required it is worth its weight in gold." If this phenomenon occurs in waters you fish, the floating snail fly fished on a greased leader is the answer.

Clams (class Pelecypoda) are most abundant in large rivers and although trout will eat young ones, I have never known such feeding to be selective.

Appendix A: Lifelike Materials

Artificials should be constructed of materials that best imitate the living appearance of the various features of the organism. Wings, for example, are often translucent yet mottled by opaque veins or cells. High quality hackle is translucent, and mixing solid colors with one of the variant types or grizzly suggests mottling. Polypropylene yarn makes excellent wings because it is translucent and slightly kinked, reflecting and transmitting light in a most lifelike way. Body materials range across the full breadth of the fly tier's imagination.

BLENDING AND DUBBING FURS

Most of my flies have dubbed fur bodies. This material is easily applied, has the translucency of life, and can be blended for any desired color.

Blended furs are better than single colors because the heather mixtures more closely ape nature's color schemes. Caucci and Nastasi have suggested that by blending red, yellow, and blue furs in correct proportions any color can be achieved. While this was once thought to be true, researchers have clearly shown that other colors must be added to successfully produce many shades. When blending furs, start with the basic color of the organism and add small amounts of related colors for highlights. To darken a particular color, add grays, black, darker components, or a darker shade of the color. To lighten a color, add creams, white, lighter components, or a lighter shade of the color. Blacks and reds are very strong colors and should be used sparingly when blended with other colors. For example, for olive, start with olive-dyed fur that is close to the final desired color. Add a little brown, a little yellow, and a little green as highlighters, more of one or the other if the final shade must be lightened or darkened. This method of blending gives a very lifelike appearance to the fly. Below are listed the basic colors with suggestions for variations.

Red: add yellow and white for warm tones; blue for cool tones
Yellow: add white for warm tones; orange for sulphur tones
Blue: add white for warm tones; gray or black for cool tones
Brown: components are red and green; red or black will darken the shade; white and tan will lighten
Olive: components are yellow, green, and brown; various hues can be arrived at by adding blue, red, yellow, green, brown, tan, or white
Purple: components are blue and red; change the shading with red, blue, white, gray
Orange: components are red and yellow; bright colors are mixed with red and yellow; russet colors with red, yellow, gray, black
Gray: components are black and white; for cool tones blend white, black, cool blues; add yellow for warm tones
Green: components are yellow and blue; warm with blue or gray; darken with gray or black

Actual blending may be done several ways. The furs may be teased apart and mixed with the fingers, an excellent technique for producing a strongly mottled effect in the fly; clumps of color will be evident in the finished mat. For insects of more uniform coloration, a finer mixing of the furs is necessary. This may be accomplished by cutting the various furs into soapy water, stirring, rinsing, then felting on a piece of window screen as Polly Rosborough recommends in his superb book *Tying and Fishing the Fuzzy Nymphs.* Blend cards available from some supply houses can also be used. However, the best method uses an automatic blender, either the kitchen variety or one of the new miniblenders. Furs may be mixed wet or dry and components easily added to bring the mat to the correct shade. Completed felts should be placed in plastic bags and labeled as to contents and finished color.

Numerous furs can be used for dubbing; muskrat, beaver, fox, mole, fitch, and rabbit are only a few of the natural hairs employed. Polypropylene plastic is now being drawn to extremely fine diameters and cut and blended into dubbing materials which are available in many colors. Of the furs with which I have experimented, domestic white rabbit has become a favorite. Easily colored with fabric dyes, it is also inexpensive and readily obtainable as entire skins or swatches. If untanned, the hair will still contain natural oils which highlight the colors. I normally obtain entire skins to take advantage of the various lengths and textures of fur on the different areas of the animal. Belly fur is exceedingly soft and fine; guard hairs on the back make the fur coarser and more translucent (these guard hairs make fine legs on nymphs); the mask has short fur; and so forth. Other nonwhite furs may be dyed to add tones, or bleached and dyed to any color. Bleaching produces excellent variations of color. One of my favorite furs for bleaching is that from the back of the common, cottontail rabbit. Gray underfur becomes a fleshy tan — a perfect match for many scuds — while the guard hairs become a mottled tan and brown. These bleached guard hairs make excellent legs for nymphs.

Another favorite of mine for blending is sparkle yarn. This material sells under a variety of trade names, but all have a slightly frosted, sparkly sheen. It's artificial seal fur if there ever was. Cut into half-inch lengths and blended with natural furs, it forms an outstanding mixture. Don't pass up a chance to add all the colors of sparkle yarn to your collection.

BLEACHING HAIRS AND FURS

In the procedures recommended by Polly Rosborough, the bleaching agent is hydrogen peroxide. Clairoxide (a Miss Clairol product) is superb for this process. Keep the swatch of hide small (about four by four inches); big pieces tend to trap air or not be exposed properly to the fluid. Place the hide in a jar and cover it with the Clairoxide. Cap loosely to permit gasses to escape. The process is relatively slow, so check the fur every eight to twelve hours until the desired shade is obtained. Rinse well in cold water and dry thoroughly. Rapid bleaching is easily accomplished if you obtain some Miss Clairol Basic White Booster from a beauty salon. Mix at a ratio of one-fourth cup booster per cup of Clairoxide. Work the mixture through the materials and watch the color fade. Be sure you wear rubber gloves; it's a potent solution. When the material is bleached to your preference, wash it well in soapy water and rinse in hot water. Brown hackle can be bleached to a pale ginger or golden ginger in twenty minutes to one hour, the speed of the process dependent upon the individual neck. The hackle shaft remains flexible with this method, whereas other methods often leave the shaft brittle. Herls, body feathers, and furs also bleach beautifully with this method. Cottontail rabbit reaches the desired tan and brown mottle in about twenty minutes to one hour, while peacock herl bleaches to a handsome tan in fifteen minutes.

DYEING MATERIALS

Dyeing materials for fly tying is no more difficult than the simple bleaching procedures described above. For furs, feathers, and wool yarns, use commercial fabric dyes such as Rit, Tintex, or Putnam's. For polypropylene yarn, acrylics, feathers, and floss bodies, use felt tip pens with permanent, aniline inks.

Poly yarns are easily dyed to color with felt tip pens. The commercially available colors of yarn can be counterdyed to produce nearly any shade. For example, a series of grays can be produced by dyeing tan, off-white, and white with a dark gray pen; tan produces a dark slate color, off-white a nice dark gray, and white a most appealing medium gray. A lighter shade of gray pen yields another series of grays. Dun (gray brown) can be produced by coloring tan yarns with a light gray pen. Mottling can be achieved by lightly dotting the marker along the yarn. Tan poly dotted with olive and brown makes a most convincing wing for the *Stenonema* mayflies. The variations are limitless, but be sure the markers contain waterproof, aniline dyes. After coloring, wait several minutes for the dye to bind with the yarn, then wipe the yarn with a clean rag to remove the excess dye.

Dyeing with fabric colors requires a little knowledge of the fur or feathers. Hard furs take the dye more slowly, bleached furs respond more quickly than naturally light furs, and so forth. The general procedure is followed by more specific recommendations.

Equipment
1. large, white enameled pot
2. kitchen tongs or large hemostat
3. large metal spoon
4. measuring spoons (one-quarter teaspoon through one tablespoon)
5. thermometer (optional)
6. hair drier or fan (optional)

Materials
1. dyes — All recommendations pertain to Rit dyes. Variations occur between brands, and if others are used they should be tested first on material scraps.
2. salt
3. cream of tartar

General Procedures
Prepare the material for dyeing by washing in a mild dish detergent solution until thoroughly wet. For swatches of hide, remove as much fat as possible from the skin before washing. As when bleaching, keep the pieces

small so they can be handled easily and take the dye properly. Just prior to dyeing, rinse the material well in hot water to remove all traces of soap.

Place the dye solution in the enameled pot and heat to boiling. Add the freshly rinsed material; rinsing in hot water will decrease the temperature differential between the dye bath and the material and hasten the dyeing operation. Stir the bath to assure exposure of all areas of the fur or feathers to the dye. Heavy furs and hackle capes should be held with the tongs and swished in the solution. Loose feathers should be bundled by tying at one end before dyeing. Yarns or monofilament are simply placed in the bath for the desired time. Once dyed, the material is removed and rinsed in tepid, running water to remove excess dye. Blot dry with a paper or cloth towel and spread the items on newspaper near a heat vent or dry with a hair drier or fan. The last method is especially good at restoring the feathers to their original shapes.

Some colors are not attainable with a single dye bath; the material must be dyed one color, then other shades are added in subsequent baths. Olive and black are two such colors. Remember to apply the weaker color first then add only a very small amount of the stronger color to the dyed material. Many interesting and excellent shades can be obtained this way.

Before committing any material to the dye pot, test the results with a small swatch or single feather. Remember, too, that the dye bath weakens with use, so don't figure on dyeing twenty hackle capes or swatches of hide in one bath. Check it after a few and add a little dye to bring it back to full strength. Also check the water level to be sure it isn't boiling away too fast, thereby increasing the concentration of dye in the bath.

Pot, tongs, spoons, and thermometers must be washed to remove all traces of dye before a different color is used. Otherwise, traces of the first dye will alter the color of the second.

The dye formulas below provide a broad selection of colors and materials. You may desire to expand upon the recipes listed here; if so, keep a notebook of the recipes you develop. Record the kind and amount of dye(s), dyeing time, amount of solution, any special additives and their amounts, and the materials dyed. Tape a piece of finished material into the book next to the formula for future reference.

White Rabbit Fur

This is an easily dyed fur that holds color well and is an excellent basic blending material. Prepare the dye bath with two quarts of water, one teaspoon of salt, and the recommended amounts of dye. Maintain the solution at the boiling point (100 degrees Celsius or 212 degrees Fahrenheit) during the dyeing process.

Color	Time	Dye
black	2 min.	1 tbsp. black, use fur previously dyed dark brown
sky blue	2 min.	1 tsp. royal blue
indigo blue	2 min.	1 tsp. marine blue
blue gray	2 min.	1 tsp. navy blue
light brown	2 min.	1 tsp. dark brown
medium brown	2 min.	1 tbsp. dark brown
dark brown	2 min.	1 tbsp. dark brown and 1 tsp. black
claret	2 min.	1 tsp. scarlet and ¼ tsp. navy
gold	2 min.	1 tsp. gold
medium gray	2 min.	1 tsp. gray
gray brown	2 min.	1 tsp. charcoal gray
dark gray	2 min.	1 tbsp. charcoal gray
grass green	2 min.	1 tsp. jade green
kelly green	2 min.	1 tbsp. jade green
dark green	2 min.	1 tbsp. jade green and 1 tsp. black
yellowish olive	2 min.	½ tsp. olive green and 1 tsp. yellow
golden olive	2 min.	½ tsp. olive green and 1 tsp. gold
olive	15 sec.	add 1 tsp. dark brown to golden olive, use fur previously dyed golden olive
olive brown	30 sec.	same as olive
light pink	2 min.	1 tsp. rose pink
dark pink	2 min.	1 tbsp. rose pink
purple	2 min.	1 tsp. purple
tangerine brown	2 min.	1 tsp. chestnut brown
red brown	2 min.	1 tbsp. chestnut brown
buffalo brown	2 min.	2 tsp. cocoa brown
golden brown	2 min.	1 tsp. gold and ½ tsp. cocoa brown
scarlet	2 min.	1 tsp. scarlet
tan	2 min.	2 tsp. tan
tangerine	2 min.	1 tsp. tangerine
pale yellow	2 min.	½ tsp. yellow
dark yellow	2 min.	1 tsp. yellow
brilliant yellow	15 min.	saturated solution of picric acid

Jet black is not possible to achieve with these fabric dyes. For this color, commercially prepared hairs dyed by an aniline process are best. The black given above is excellent for blending or as a pastel black dubbing.

Flat Monofilament

Nylon takes Rit dyes surprisingly fast. For mono use the same baths as indicated for white rabbit, but cut the time to fifteen *seconds.* Dye nylon stockings this way, too.

Hackle Capes, Mallard Flank Feathers, Bird Body Feathers, Bleached Herl, Bleached Furs, Natural Fiber Yarns, Other Soft-bodied Materials

The solutions and times recommended for white rabbit work for these materials, also. For feathers, dyeing time may need to be reduced to one minute. Check the bath with a single feather first, before committing the entire lot or cape.

Deer Hair, Calf Tail, and Other Hard Hairs

This group requires a different approach because these hairs resist binding with the dye. However, once dyed they hold the color very well and are widely useful. During experiments with these materials I tried large amounts of dye and salt, vinegar added to the bath and other techniques that gave hit and miss results. Much more satisfactory was the addition of various mordants, or dye-fixers. This process is quite rapid and therefore does not cause damage to the hair or degradation of the hide in any way.

Deer hair is a basic material for many fly patterns and several shades are required. The dyes given below will yield a good working selection. In addition, by choosing hair from different portions of the hide, different effects can be achieved with each dye. In general, hair from the back is dark gray, from the sides medium to pale gray, and from the belly white. For the widest range of colors, dye a piece of hide from each region with each color. Don't attempt to dye patches larger than four by four inches, or the dye will not penetrate the interior hairs. Wash each swatch gently in a mild detergent solution and rinse thoroughly before dyeing. During the actual dyeing process, hold the swatch with the tongs and agitate continually to assure proper penetration of the solution to all the hairs. Calf tail, squirrel tail, raccoon tail, and other comparable hard hairs are dyed with the same

Color	Time	Dye
black	2 min.	1 tbsp. black, use hair previously dyed dark brown
dark brown	2 min.	1 tbsp. dark brown and 1 tsp. black
green	2 min.	1 tbsp. jade green
olive	2 min.	2 tsp. gold and 1 tsp. olive green
red brown	2 min.	1 tbsp. cocoa
tan	2 min.	1 tbsp. tan
yellow	2 min.	1 tbsp. yellow

formulas, but require three to five minutes of dyeing time. Prepare the dye bath with two quarts of water, one teaspoon of salt, and one teaspoon of cream of tartar (the mordant).

Again, as for rabbit fur, the black is more pastel than commercially prepared hairs, but nevertheless is usable for most purposes.

Photodyeing

This is a special process to achieve a gray color in hackle capes and involves the use of photographic compounds. This technique was described in Eric Leiser's excellent book *Fly Tying Materials.* Brown capes bleached to a cream or pale ginger shade can be dyed to fine shades of dun gray, and the color produced is very stable.

The necks are soaked in a solution of silver nitrate for at least one hour: for a light gray tint, one-eighth ounce of silver nitrate in two quarts of water; for medium gray, three-eighths ounce in two quarts of water; and for dark gray, five-eighths ounce of silver nitrate to two quarts of water. Agitate the necks every fifteen minutes. Remove the necks from the silver nitrate solution one at a time and allow them to drain until the excess fluid has been removed. Next, place them in Dektol developer for one minute; this will develop the color. Agitate the necks to coat all parts of the feathers. Remove from the Dektol, drain briefly, and transfer to a stop bath for one minute. Agitate continually while they are in the stop bath. Remove and drain and place in a fixer for ten minutes, then wash in running water for twenty minutes. Blot dry between folds of newspaper and dry them with a hair drier. Be careful when transferring the necks not to get the solution from any one bath into the *previous* bath. It's best to have a separate set of tongs for each bath; when transferring the necks, be careful not to let the tongs touch the solution of the next bath.

This technique can also be used to superimpose the gray on other dyed colors. By photodyeing colored necks or by using photographic toners, many interesting shades can be produced.

STRIPPING PEACOCK HERL

Stripped peacock herl is widely used for fly bodies in natural and dyed colors. The best quill is found in the "eye" of the tail feather. To remove the fiber from the quill, place the entire eye in a shallow pan of liquid laundry bleach (such as Clorox) and agitate gently, watching closely. When the fiber is totally removed, rinse in cold water and place the eye in a bath of baking soda (sodium bicarbonate) to neutralize the bleach. Agitate for a minute or two. Rinse thoroughly in cold water and dry. The dye solutions recommended for white rabbit work well on this material at one minute.

Appendix B: Dressings

The imitations in this appendix are arranged by chapter and in the order of their discussion. Most of the tying procedures are well known, but in the few instances of less familiar ones, tying notes are added. Tying methods and dressings should not be considered absolute; feel free to experiment.

Through the years I have worked with many hook styles in an attempt to select as few as possible for all my tying requirements. For standard-length hooks, I have come to prefer Mustad quality 94840, fine wire, TDTE in sizes through 16; for #18 through #28, Mustad 94842, fine wire, TUTE. For longer flies I use Mustad 9672, 3XL, TDTE. Occasionally a 2XL hook is best (Mustad 9671) or an up-eyed salmon fly hook may be needed (Mustad 36890). Tying length for these hooks can be varied slightly depending upon the particular pattern: standard length is from the eye to a position directly above the point of the barb; extended length is from the eye to a point one-quarter of the way around the hook bend. For dry flies the body is tied standard length; for many nymphs and larvae the extended length can be used. I prefer light wire hooks because they penetrate the fish's mouth tissues more easily. If weight is desired, it is added in the form of lead or copper wire wrappings on the shank.

For thread I use prewaxed Danville or Monochord. Danville's is best for flies #10 and smaller. The heavier Monochord works best on flies larger than #10. Color matches the body except for special effects. Such exceptions are noted.

Standard and Extended Lengths for Recommended Hooks			
Hook	Size	Standard Length (mm)	Extended Length (mm)
94840	2	21	24
	4	19	21
	6	17	19
	8	14	16
	10	11	12
	12	10	11
	14	9	10
	16	7	8
94842	18	6	7
	20	5	6
	22	4.5	5
	24	4	4.5
	26	3.5	4
	28	3	3.5
9672	2	33	37
	4	26	29
	6	22	24
	8	18	20
	10	16	18
	12	14	15.5
	14	12	13.5
	16	9.5	10.5
	18	8	9

Mayflies

Strip Nymph

Hook: 94840, #6 to #10

Abdomen: Strip of tanned hide with fur on (cut 1/16 to 3/16 inch wide depending on fly size), tan color most used

Thorax: Dubbed fur applied on a dubbing loop

Legs: Guard hairs or calf tail hairs (insert in dubbing loop after dubbing is applied and at right angles to thread of loop, close loop, twist tight)

Wing Case: Peacock herl pulled tight over top of thorax

Fig. B–1. Strip nymph

Red Brown Nymph

Hook: 94840 and 94842, #6 to #20

Tail: Pheasant tail fibers, rusty brown

Abdomen: Fur dubbing dyed buffalo brown — see appendix A — or yarn of correct shade

Thorax: Fur dubbing, buffalo brown, applied on dubbing loop

Legs: Guard hairs from back of bleached cottontail rabbit hide (see appendix A), apply dubbing to one side of dubbing loop, insert hairs at right angles to thread of loop (fig. B–2), close loop and twist tight to form chenille that is wrapped forward to form thorax and legs

Wing Case: Peacock herl pulled tight over top of thorax

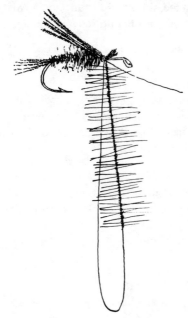

Fig. B–2. Red Brown Nymph showing dubbing loop with guard hairs inserted

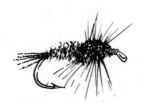

Fig. B–3. Finished Red Brown Nymph

Sawyer's Pheasant Tail

Hook: 94840 and 94842, #14 to #22
Tail: Tips of pheasant tail fibers that are used to form body
Body: Pheasant tail fibers, rusty brown
Wing Case: Pheasant tail fibers. After wrapping fibers forward to form body, tie off at head then fold back over thorax, wrap down with thread and fold forward. Repeat as necessary to build up prominent wing case.

Wet/Dry Fly

Hook: 94840 and 94842, #10 to #24
Tail: None, or one may be used if fly is tied stillborn style
Body: Dubbing or unwaxed silk thread (buttonhole twist)
Hackle: Feather from shoulder of wing (covert feather)

Extended-Body Para-Drake

Hook: 94840, #4 to #10
Tail: Pheasant tail fibers
Body: Deer hair, extended back beyond hook for length equal to that of shank, pale yellow and rusty brown most used
Wing: Clump of deer hair tied in at thorax after body is formed
Hackle: Wound parachute style around base of wing

Variant

Hook: 94840 and 94842, all sizes
Tail: Stiff fibers from hackle feather or stiff guard hairs
Body: Dubbed fur
Hackle: Good quality dry fly hackle of color to match wings of natural

Poly-Dun

Hook: 94840 and 94842, #8 to #18
Tail: Stiff hackle fibers or guard hairs, split into V shape
Body: Dubbed fur
Wing: Clump of polypropylene yarn or sparkle yarn tied upright at thorax
Hackle: Wound parachute style around base of wing, color to match wing

Loop Wing

Hook: 94842, #20 to #28
Tail: Hackle fibers
Body: Dubbed fur
Hackle: Wound over thorax and trimmed flat on bottom
Wing: Mallard flank feather fibers tied in at rear of thorax and looped forward to form upright wing, tied off at head

Poly-Spinner

Hook: 94840 and 94842, #16 to #28
Tail: Hackle fibers
Body: Dubbed fur
Wings: Polypropylene yarn tied crossways to the shank at the thorax; keep the wing very thin and filmy by using only a few fibers of yarn

Hackle-Wing Spinner

Hook: 94840, #8 to #16
Tail: Hackle fibers
Body: Dubbed fur or extended deer hair
Wings: Good quality hackle wound figure-eight style over thorax and trimmed top and bottom

Hair-Wing Spinner

Hook: 94840, #4 to #10
Tail: Pheasant tail fibers
Body: Deer hair, extended
Wings: Clump of calf tail hair tied in at thorax, separated into two wings which are pulled to sides and held in place with figure-eight wraps of thread

Stoneflies

Mono Stonefly Nymph

Hook: 9672, sizes as below
Tails: Two quills from leading edge of primary wing feather of goose, tied one on either side of hook and spread
Foundation: Lead wire set at sides of hook and well secured; for unweighted versions use monofilament
Underbody: Floss
Abdomen: Flat monofilament or Swannundaze
Thorax: Dubbed fur or yarn, well picked out to simulate gills
Legs: Hair, as listed below
Wing Pads: Section of turkey feather
Tying Notes: Tie in tails, foundation, flat mono, and floss in that order; wind floss over foundation and tie off at head. Lacquer and permit to dry; wind flat mono over rear half of fly and tie off; tie in turkey feather section, form a leg chenille (see Red Brown Nymph); wrap chenille a turn or two and tie off; hold turkey section back over abdomen and crimp it a short ways behind the thorax; fold forward and tie down to

WORKING PATTERNS FOR MONO STONEFLY NYMPHS
Eastern and Midwestern U. S.

	Giant Black Stonefly (Pteronarcys dorsata)	Family Perlidae, genus Paragnetina	Family Perlidae, other genera, especially Acroneuria
Hook Size:	2–8	6–10	6–10
Thread:	dark brown	same as underbody	orange
Tails:	black	black	orangish brown
Underbody:	black or dark brown	yellow or tan, dyed black on top with felt tip pen	amber, mottled with brown felt tip pen
Mono:	clear or pale gray	clear, tan, or pale gray	tan or pale gray
Thorax:	brown and cream	tan or yellow and white	orangish brown and white
Legs:	black calf tail	black calf tail	natural cottontail rabbit guard hairs
Wing Pads:	dark turkey	dark turkey	light turkey dyed with yellow-brown felt tip pen

WORKING PATTERNS FOR MONO STONEFLY NYMPHS
Western U. S.

	Giant Salmon Fly (Pteronarcys californica)	Black Willow Fly (Acroneuria nigrita)	Golden Stonefly (Acroneuria californica)
Hook:	2–8	6–10	6–10
Thread:	black	black	orange
Tails:	black	black	orangish brown
Underbody:	pink, dyed black on top with felt tip pen	black	amber
Mono:	pale gray	black	gold
Thorax:	black and white	black and white	gold and white
Legs:	black calf tail	black calf tail	cottontail rabbit guard hairs dyed gold
Wing Pads:	dark turkey	dark turkey	light turkey dyed with yellow-brown felt tip pen

Note: The general *Acroneuria* pattern given for the eastern U. S. is also applicable to the West

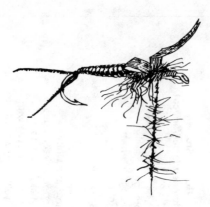

Fig. B–4. Mono Stonefly Nymph with first wing pad formed

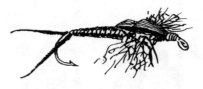

Fig. B–5. Finished Mono Stonefly Nymph

form hindwing pads (fig. B–4); repeat to form front half of thorax (fig. B–5).

Hair Wing Stonefly (adult)

Hook: 9672, sizes as below
Tail: Clump of woodchuck hair tied short
Abdomen: Fur chenille — form dubbing loop, cut hair from hide, insert in loop at right angles to thread, twist tight, trim to shape
Thorax: Fur dubbing palmered with two hackles trimmed top and bottom
Wing: Woodchuck hair with guard hairs; other tan, mottled hairs also work
Head: Dubbed fur palmered with two hackles trimmed top and bottom

Caddisflies

Blonde Burlap

Hook: 94840 or 94842, #2 to #20
Tail: Honey-colored feather fibers

Working Patterns for Hair Wing Stoneflies

Insect	Region	Hook	Body	Hackle
Perlidae (amber stoneflies)	E,M,W	6–8	pastel orange	brown
Giant Black Stonefly	E,M	2–6	yellow/black mottle	black
Willow Flies	E,M,W	8–10	golden olive	black
Golden Stonefly	W	6–8	gold	brown
Salmon Fly	W	2–6	salmon pink	black

Body: Burlap bleached to creamy white, tied in and twisted while wound to form segmented body, picked out well

Hackle: Soft feather of honey color

Mono Caddis Larva

Hook: 94840, #8 to #14, for curved body use Mustad 37160

Underbody: Floss; most-used colors are green, olive, gray

Abdomen: Flat monofilament (twelve-pound test), colored as underbody

Rib: Tag end of tying thread

Gills: Ostrich herl (white) tied in at thorax and pointing back under abdomen, secured to underside of abdomen with rib

Thorax: Dubbing

Legs: Guard hairs (spin chenille with dubbing loop)

Sparkle Caddis Pupa

Hook: 94840 and 94842, #8 to #20

Body: Blended sparkle yarn, dubbed on and well picked out

Rib: Tinsel

Wing Pads: Optional; body feather trimmed to shape, set one on each side, pointing down and back

Hackle: Soft body feather

Note: Pupa colored similar to adults

Devil Bug Caddis Emerger

Hook: 94840 and 94842, #8 to #20

Tail: Tips of deer hair used for body

Body: Deer hair folded over top of hook: tie in at rear of hook, wrap thread forward over hair to head, fold hair back over *top* of shank, wrap thread back over it then forward again, fold hair forward and tie down at head

Hackle: Butt ends of hair used to form body, trimmed to one-half length of body

Poly-Caddis

Hook: 94840, #8 to #16
Abdomen: Dubbed fur
Thorax: Dubbed fur overwound with dry fly hackle trimmed top and bottom
Wing: Polypropylene yarn or sparkle yarn; apply heavily, trim butt end so a small clump is left sticking up, apply head cement to clump and tying thread

Micro-Poly-Caddis

Hook: 94842, #18 to #28
Body: Dubbed fur
Wing: Poly yarn
Legs: Butt end of wing split and tied outward at sides, trim to length of body and remove all but ten or so fibers from each side

Working Patterns for Poly-Caddis and Micro-Poly-Caddis			
Hook	*Body*	*Wing*	*Hackle*
14–28	gray	blue gray	dark gray
12–28	brown	dark brown	dark brown
8–18	orange	rusty brown	rusty brown
8–28	yellow	ginger	ginger
12–18	green	white	badger
14–28	black	black	black

Midges

South Platte Brassy

Hook: 94840 or 94842, #14 to #20
Thread: Fluorescent red
Body: Bright copper wire, twenty-six to thirty gauge depending on hook size, wound in one smooth layer
Throat: a few rusty brown feather fibers

Midge Nymph

Hook: 94840 or 94842, #14 to #24
Body: Dubbed fur (use half sparkle yarn in blend); most used colors are black, gray, pale yellow, and gray brown; build up into fat cigar shape

Hatching Midge Pupa (imitates larger species)

Hook: 94840, #8 to #16
Tail: Poly yarn (white)
Body: Dubbed fur ribbed with buttonhole twist thread; thorax robust and unribbed
Legs and Wing Pads: Clump of feather fibers tied at throat
Thoracic Gills: Poly yarn (white) tied in like spinner wings (keep short)

Horse Collar Midge

Hook: 94840 or 94842, #14 to #24
Tail: Several feather fibers, tied short
Abdomen: Unwaxed buttonhole thread (silk)
Thorax: Chenille, peacock herl, or dubbing; robust

Griffith's Gnat

Hook: 94840 or 94842, #14 to #28
Body: Peacock herl or fur dubbing
Hackle: Palmered; grizzly, dun, or brown; trim top and bottom for picky fish

Midge Variant

Hook: 94840 or 94842, #14 to #28
Tail: Hackle fibers, stiff
Body: Tying thread or very thin dubbing; colors most used are gray, brown, black, and pale yellow
Hackle: Dry fly quality, shade to match body

Cranefly Larva

Hook: 9672, #4 to #14
Body: Coarse dubbing (use dubbing loop) or fuzzy yarns; robust
Rib: As below

Working Patterns for Cranefly Larva

Thread	Body	Rib
gray	off-white	flat mono dyed dark gray
tan	tan	copper wire
olive	dark green	silver wire
gray	blue gray	flat mono dyed dark gray
orange	dingy orange	copper wire

Troth Skater

Hook: 94840, #6 to #14
Hackle: Elk body hair; tie in clump at rear of hook with tips pointing forward, push hairs backward and outward to form hackle at rear of hook, wrap thread in front of hair to help prop it up; wind thread forward and repeat at head of fly

March Fly

Hook: 94840, #14 and #16
Abdomen: Black dubbing; robust
Thorax: Red or yellow dubbing; short and robust
Wings: Black poly yarn tied delta style

Damsels, Dragons, and Bugs

Damselfly Nymph

Hook: 94840, #8 to #14
Abdomen and Gills: Sparce clump of marabou tied in at bend of hook; length one and one-half times length of hook shank
Thorax: Fur, applied heavily on dubbing loop; wind hook shank with lead wire before winding on thorax; the lead wire will cause the fly to move with a jigging action when it is retrieved, this motion will activate the marabou abdomen to give an excellent lifelike motion to the fly
Legs: Guard hairs inserted in dubbing loop
Wing Pads: Peacock herl pulled over top of thorax
Colors: Olive tan, olive brown, gray brown, purple brown

Hair-Wing Damsel

Hook: Mustad 94840, #8 to #12
Body: Deer hair; extended
Hind Wings: Calf tail hair; tied delta fashion
Fore Wings: Hackle, trimmed top and bottom
Most Used Colors: (fore wing/hind wing/body) *Males:* grizzly/white/bright blue, black/black/emerald green, grizzly/white/ruby; *Females:* grizzly/white/olive-tan, grizzly/white/yellow-brown

Assam Dragon

Hook: 9672, #6 to #10
Body: Strip of hide with fur left on, one-sixteenth to one-eighth inch wide, tie in at bend and wrap forward in close turns; weight body with lead wire before applying fur
Hackle: Soft, bird body feather; fibers should be as long as hook shank

Carey Special

Hook: 94840, #2 to #10
Body: Peacock or ostrich herl, chenille, or dubbing; very bulky and weighted
Hackle: Soft, bird body feathers, tied full

Muskrat Nymph

Hook: 94840, #2 to #20
Tail: Coot body fibers
Body: Blend of gray furs to yield medium-dark color
Hackle: Coot feather

Fur Chenille Dragon

Hook: 9671 (2XL), #2 to #8
Abdomen: Fur chenille trimmed to shape
Thorax: Dubbed fur
Legs: Guard hairs or calf tail
Wing Pads: Peacock herl pulled over top of thorax

Waterboatman, Backswimmer, Giant Waterbug

Hook: 94840, #10 to #16; for giant waterbug 9672, #4 to #10
Body: Blended sparkle yarn, applied on dubbing loop and well picked out
Rib: Silver tinsel
Overlay: Section of turkey or goose feather, tied in at rear of body, pulled over top, and secured at head
Hackle: Soft, body feather; fibers as long as hook shank

Jassid

Hook: 94840 or 94842, #16 to #28
Body: Closely palmered hackle trimmed top and bottom
Wing: Small body feather lacquered with head cement and set in over top of body, downwing style

Wooly Worm Larvae

Hair-Leg Wooly Worm

Hook: 9672, #2 to #18
Tail: Feather fibers or hair, tied short
Abdomen: Coarse dubbing (use dubbing loop) or fuzzy yarns, well picked out, wound on rear two-thirds of shank
Rib: Copper wire on lighter colored bodies, silver wire on darker bodies
Thorax: Coarse dubbing or fuzzy yarns on dubbing loop
Legs: Calf tail hair or guard hairs

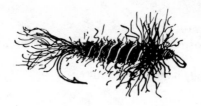

Fig. B–6. Finished Hair–Leg Wooly Worm

Crowe Beetle

Hook: 94840 or 94842, #8 to #20
Body: Fur dubbing
Wing Cases (elytra): Deer hair tied in at rear of hook and folded over top of body, secured at head
Legs: Several hairs from wing cases spread to each side and trimmed to length

Marinaro's Beetle

Tied the same way as the Jassid

Poly-Beetle

Hook: Mustad 94840 and 94842, #10 to #28
Body: Dubbed fur overwound with closely palmered hackle trimmed top and bottom
Wing Cases (elytra): Poly yarn tied in at rear of hook, folded forward over top of body, and secured at head; trim butt end of wing as for Poly-Caddis; use enough yarn for a bulky look; don't pull yarn completely tight along top of body, allow it to be just a little loose to get greater bulk and provide more air spaces

Egger's June Bug

Hook: 94840, #4 to #8
Body: Spun deer hair, trimmed to shape
Hackle: Palmered, trimmed top and bottom
Wing Cases (elytra): Optional; poly yarn tied in at rear and pulled over top of fly

Polish Warbonnet

Hook: 94840, #2 to #8
Tail: Clump of deer body hair, tied short
Body: Spun deer hair, trimmed to full shape

Wing: Clump of deer body hair tied over back
Head: Wing butt, trimmed to full Muddler shape

Inchworm

Hook: 9672, #10 to #14
Body: Spun deer hair, trimmed cylindrical; green, yellow, or tan

The Ant and the Grasshopper

Para-Ant (worker)

Hook: 94840 or 94842, sizes as below
Abdomen (gaster): Dubbed fur
Waist (pedicel): Thread
Head and Thorax: Dubbed fur, on #14 and larger use two separate clumps
     of dubbing; on #16 and smaller one clump of dubbing serves as both
     head and thorax
Hackle: Parachute style; use quill from leading edge (short side) of goose
     primary feather for post around which hackle is wound, trim post
     flush with hackle after winding and put dot of head cement on
     trimmed post

Working Patterns for Para-Ant			
Natural	*Hook*	*Body*	*Hackle*
black	10–22	black	black
red and black	12–22	abdomen black, thorax rusty red	rusty brown
red	14–24	rusty red	rusty brown
brown	16–24	dark brown	furnace
amber/yellow	16–24	clay yellow	ginger

Winged Ant (upright wing)

Tie as for Para-Ant but replace feather shaft with clump of feather fibers,
poly yarn, or calf tail hair to simulate wings

Spent Ant

Ant-style body with poly yarn wing tied in crossways to the hook at the
pedicel; keep the yarn sparce so fly will lie in the film

Wet Ant

Ant-style body with thread and lacquer. Use soft hackle tied full at head

Grasshopper

Hook: 9672, #8 to #14
Tail: Clump of woodchuck guard hairs, tied short
Body: Fur chenille; golden yellow has universal appeal; in some areas a chartreuse body is more effective
Underwing: Clump of yellow deer body hair
Overwing: Mottled turkey feather segment lacquered with vinyl cement
Head: Spun deer hair, trimmed cylindrical
Legs: Deer hair tied in for head and left untrimmed at back and sides of head

Cricket

Same as Grasshopper except all black

The Non-insects

Hair Leg Scud

Hook: 94840, #8 to #16
Tail: End of overlay
Body: Bleached cottontail rabbit fur for tan color, others are olive or gray; weighted if desired
Rib: Copper or silver wire
Overlay: Wood duck flank or tan-dyed mallard for tan fly; gray or olive for others; tie in at head and fold back over body, secure by winding with wire (figs. B–7, B–8)

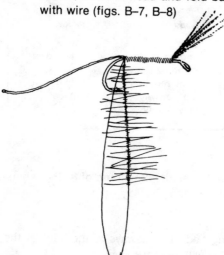

Fig. B–7. Hair Leg Scud showing overlay tied in at head and dubbing loop with guard hairs inserted

Fig. B–8. Finished Hair Leg Scud

Legs: Guard hairs; for tan scud use bleached cottontail rabbit, for others use guard hairs from dyed white rabbit fur

Cressbug

Hook: 94840, #12 to #16
Body: Coarsely dubbed fur (leave in guard hairs), well picked out, trimmed flat top and bottom
Overlay: Feather segment of correct color
Rib: Copper or silver wire

Crayfish (realistic approach)

Hook: 9672, #6 to #14
Chelipeds (pincers): Two clumps of bleached cottontail rabbit fur with guard hairs left in, tied in at bend of hook, each clump wrapped extended-body style along the basal half; the formed chelipeds should extend rearward from the bend of the hook in a V
Cephalothorax (head and thorax which in crayfish are fused): Bleached cottontail rabbit fur coarsely applied on dubbing loop; lacquered section of mottled turkey feather pulled over top; weighted with lead wire.
Legs: Guard hairs from bleached cottontail rabbit fur placed in dubbing loop
Abdomen: Bleached cottontail rabbit fur, dubbed
Telson (tail fan): Clump of bleached cottontail rabbit fur with guard hairs left in; tied forward over eye of hook and spread to fan shape; trim to length
Note: Other colors may be used to more closely match the naturals in your home waters

Crayfish (impressionistic approach)

Hook: 9672, #6 to #14
Tail: Thin clump of brown bucktail or craft fur
Body: Gold tinsel, weighted with lead wire
Wing: Orange, olive green, and brown bucktail or craft fur layered with brown on top, tied like a streamer wing
Throat: Clump of olive, tan, brown, or gold marabou same length as hook, tied pointing *forward* under eye of hook; when the fly is retrieved with a pulsing motion this throat will bend back under the hook and imitate the chopping motion of the natural's tail

Gray Ghost

Hook: 9672, #2 to #14
Body: Orange floss ribbed with silver tinsel

Wing: Gray hackle feathers
Throat: White bucktail, peacock herl, and gold pheasant crest
Shoulder: Silver pheasant body feather

Blacknose Dace

Hook: 9672, #2 to #14
Body: Silver tinsel
Wing: Bucktail or acrylic craft fur, layered white (on bottom), black, and brown
Throat: Small clump of fluorescent red craft fur

Mickey Finn

Same as Blacknose Dace except wing is yellow, red, yellow

Mylar Minnow

Any streamer or bucktail pattern with mylar tinsel added in wing; cut tinsel into short lengths and tie in to give flash

Maribou Streamer

Any body pattern; wing is maribou feather of whatever color pattern calls for

Matuka

Hook: 9672, #2 to #14
Body: Yarn
Rib: Silver or copper wire
Wing: Six hen hackle feathers tied in at head and secured along body with rib, extending back beyond hook for a distance equal to length of hook shank; when wrapping rib, be careful not to wrap down the fibers of the wing feather
Hackle: Optional; soft hen hackle

Blonde

Hook: 94840, #2 to #6; 36890, #3/0 to #2
Tail: Clump of bucktail or acrylic craft fur, tied long
Body: Tinsel
Wing: Clump of bucktail or acrylic craft fur tied as long as tail

Muddler Minnow

Hook: 9672, #2 to #14
Tail: Mottled turkey
Body: Gold tinsel
Wing: Woodchuck hair with mottled turkey sections at each side

Head: Spun deer hair trimmed to cone shape; leave hairs at rear of head untrimmed to form skirt over body and wing

San Juan Worm

Hook: 9672, #8 to #12
Body: Bright yellowish amber chenille with short waist of fluorescent red floss

Strip Leech

Hook: 36890 (up-eyed salmon hook), #2/0 to #6
Tail: Maroon, olive, black, yellow, gold, orange or white maribou, tied sparcely
Body: Dubbed fur, gray, brown, or black
Rib: Silver wire
Wing: Strip of tanned hide with fur on, one-sixteenth to three-sixteenth inch wide depending on hook size, secured at head and ribbed against body Matuka-style; gray, brown, and black most used
Hackle: Soft, body feather, full; fibers as long as hook shank

Wet Snail

Hook: 94840, #4 to #10
Body: Gray-green wool, cone-shaped
Rib: Copper or silver wire
Hackle: Grouse

Floating Snail

Hook: 94840, #4 to #10
Body: Cork, conical shaped, overwound with partially stripped peacock herl

Tadpolly

Hook: 94840, #8 to #14
Tail: Three black hackle feathers about same length as hook
Body: Black dubbing
Head: Peacock herl, tied very full

Dam Mouse

Hook: 36890, #2 to #4/0
Tail: Grizzly hackle feathers
Body: Clump of calf tail hair just ahead of tails tied in like a skirt; remainder of body made of spun caribou body hair; trim to shape, forming ears and leaving ample caribou hair to form full skirt ahead of calf tail hair

Glossary

Abdomen: The rear portion of the body. In aquatic insects this portion consists of nine or ten segments; in crustaceans the number varies.

Anal Cell (of stonefly wing): A large cell located near the inner, rear margin of the wing

Anal Leg (of caddis): Two fleshy prolegs (which see) at the terminal end of the abdomen of a caddis larva. These anal legs bear claws and vary widely in shape from shortened and thickened structures to elongated ones.

Anal Region (of wing): The inner, rear area of the wing

Apex (apical end or apical half) Pointed; in gill referring to pointed, terminal end of gill

Behavioral Drift: Downstream movement of organisms brought about by their voluntarily leaving the bottom and drifting free in the currents (a behavioral phenomenon)

Binomial Name: The scientific name of an organism; consists of the genus and species designation for the organism, e.g., *Hexagenia limbata* (Giant Michigan Mayfly)

Catastrophic Drift: The downstream displacement of organisms by the current brought about by catastrophic events such as flood, chemical pollution, or drought

Cell (of wing): The small spaces bounded by the veins on the surface of an insect's wing

Cephalothorax (of crustaceans): "Head-thorax"; a single body region of many crustaceans formed by fusion of head and thorax

Claspers: Fingerlike structures at the terminal end of the abdomen of certain male insects used to hold the female during mating

Claw (of leg): A curved or hooked structure sometimes forked which occurs at the end of the leg of insects; used for gripping; not considered to be a segment of the tarsus

Cone: The light-sensitive cells of the eye that perceive color

Constant Drift: The random downstream displacement of organisms by the current; never involves large numbers of organisms and is not due to behavioral patterns or catastrophies

Coxa: The first segment of an insect's leg; attaches the leg to the body

Cross Veins (of wing): The thickened supporting structures of an insect's wing that extend crossways between the long veins (which see)

Cubital Region (of wing): That region of an insect's wing occurring at the inner rear corner of the wing

Detritivore: An organism that feeds on rotted plant or animal material

Detritus: Rotted plant or animal material; debris

Diurnal: Occurring in the daytime; opposite of nocturnal

Dun: The adult mayfly that hatches from the nymphal husk; the sexually immature adult mayfly; subimago

Emerger: Any adult insect during the time from which it begins to emerge from the immature husk until its wings are hardened for flight; applied to those aquatic insects that emerge in the surface film

Exoskeleton: The external, hard covering that serves as a skeleton for insects, crustaceans, and other arthropods

Femur: The third segment of an insect's leg; usually long, broad, and quite stout. Segments are numbered beginning with the one closest to the body.

Gills: Respiratory structures of aquatic organisms; may be feathery, paddle-shaped, oval, branched, or otherwise; absorb dissolved oxygen from the water and release carbon dioxide

Glossae: A pair of lobes at the apex of the labium (which see) between the paraglossae (which see)

Gnathopod: "Jaw foot"; the front legs of the scuds (Amphipoda) and cressbugs (Isopoda) used for holding food materials during feeding

Instar: The period of time between successive molts of an insect, crustacean, or other arthropod

Intercallary Veins (of wing): Veins inserted in the wing between long veins (which see); not attached to the long veins

Labium: The lower lip of an insect's mouth; may be variously specialized

Larva: The first immature stage in the life cycle of insects having a complete metamorphosis (see metamorphosis)

Life Cycle: The entire sequence of events in the development of an organism from egg to adult

Long Veins (of wing): The thickened supporting structures of an insect's wing that extend outward from the root of the wing to its edge

Mandibles: The upper or outer jaws of an insect

Metamorphosis: Changing form; in the life cycle it refers to the change in form that takes place with the development of successive stages. For insects there are three basic types of metamorphosis: (1) Gradual; the egg produces a nymph which looks like a miniature adult, it goes through several instars each time getting bigger until it eventually becomes an adult. (2) Incomplete: the egg produces a nymph (or naiad) that looks nothing like the adult, the nymph goes through several instars, and in the last instar an adult forms inside the nymphal skin, the adult then ruptures the nymphal skin and emerges. (3) Complete; the egg gives rise to a wormlike larva which goes through several instars and then enters a pupal stage, the pupa serves as a chamber in which the adult takes form, at completion of its formation the adult bursts the pupal husk and emerges.

Millimeter: A unit of linear measurement in the metric system; there are 25.4 millimeters (mm) per inch; there are 10 millimeters per centimeter (cm), and 1,000 millimeters per meter (M). A meter is 1/10,000,000 of the distance from the equator to the North Pole

Monochromatic: A light of only one color

Nocturnal: Occurring at night; opposite diurnal

Nymph: The immature stage in the life cycle of insects having a gradual or incomplete metamorphosis (see metamorphosis)

Ocelli: A simple eye (not compound)

Omnivore: An organism that feeds on plant and animal material

Oviposit: To lay eggs

Paraglossae: A pair of lobed structures at the outer, apical margin of the labium (which see)

Parasite: An organism that feeds on the living body of another organism

Penes: The genital structures of male insects

Pharate Adult: An adult insect just before emerging and still enclosed in a pupal husk

Prementum: The terminal portion of the labium (which see)

Proboscis: The tubular feeding structure of certain insects such as mosquitoes

Proleg: A fleshy protuberance that looks like a leg but that lacks joints of a true leg; occurs on some larval insects

Pupa: The second stage in the life cycle of insects that undergo complete metamorphosis (see metamorphosis)

Respiratory Tube (of fishfly larva): Paired tubes on the upper surface of the ninth abdominal segment of fishfly larva

Rods: Light-sensitive cells of the eye that perceive faint light; do not perceive colors

Sclerotized: Hardened; heavily thickened

Spacing Hump (of caddis): A fleshy protuberance that may occur on the top and sides of the first segment of the abdomen of caddis larva; used by the larva to maintain a space between its body and its case

Spinner: Sexually mature stage of mayfly adult; emerges from dun; imago

spp.: Species; used when referring to all or several species of a given genus

Stillborn: An adult aquatic insect that has been unable to entirely complete the emergence sequence and drowns

Tarsus: The fifth segment of an insect's leg. Segments are numbered starting with the one closest to the body.

Telson: The most posterior portion of the body of a crustacean; bears the anus. In the scuds (Amphipoda) the telson is small; in the cressbugs (Isopoda) the telson and the last four abdominal segments are fused; in the crayfish (Decapoda) the telson is broad and flattened and used as an aid in swimming.

Teneral Adult (of Odonata): The adult dragonfly or damselfly that is capable of flight but has not achieved full adult coloration or a fully hardened exoskeleton (which see)

Thorax: The middle section of the body; in insects consists of three segments and bears the wings and three pairs of legs (one pair per segment); in many crustaceans is fused with the head to form the cephalothorax (which see)

Tibia: The fourth segment of an insect's leg; usually long and slender. Segments are numbered beginning with the one closest to the body.

Trochanter: The second segment of an insect's leg; this segment is quite small. Segments are numbered beginning with the one closest to the body.

Veinlets: Very short, narrow veins that sometimes occur around the margin of an insect's wing

Wing Pads: Sacklike extensions of the exoskeleton (which see) that occur on the top of the second and often the third segment of the thorax of nymphs and pupa (which see) and that contain the developing wings of the adult

Annotated Bibliography

Almy, Gerald. 1978. *Tying and Fishing Terrestrials*. Harrisburg, PA: Stackpole Books. A very fine book devoted entirely to identifying, imitating, and fishing terrestrials.

Atherton, John. (1951) 1971 edition. *The Fly and the Fish*. Rockville Centre, NY: Freshet Press. A classic in American fly fishing literature. This text established the modern concepts of impressionism in fly fishing.

Bashline, L. James. 1973. *Night Fishing for Trout*. Rockville Centre, NY: Freshet Press. An easily read text with good instructions on after dark angling. Includes some delightful fishing stories and interesting history.

Blanton, Dan. 1979. "Sinking Lines for Stillwater Trout." *Fly Fisherman* 10, 6:34–39. A very good discussion on the use of various sinking lines in lakes.

Borger, Gary A. 1979. *Nymphing*. Harrisburg, PA: Stackpole Books. Discusses equipment, physiology of trout, reading the water, and relates this information to various nymphing tactics in lakes and streams. Includes information on identifying naturals and tying artificials.

Brooks, Charles. 1974. *The Trout and the Stream*. New York: Crown Publishers. The best of Brooks's three books, this is a superb discussion of where trout are found and why.

———. 1976. *Nymph Fishing for Larger Trout*. New York: Crown Publishers. A fine book on nymphing in western waters. Best for its discussion of fishing for large trout with big flies. Good information on aquatic organisms in western waters.

Burt, William H. 1957. *Mammals of the Great Lakes Region*. Ann Arbor: University of

Michigan Press. Although regional in scope, this book contains good discussions of the biology of many mammals that have a transcontinental range.

Caucci, Al and Nastasi, Bob. 1975. *Hatches.* New York: Comparahatch. The single best book on mayflies that has been written for the angler. Excellent photographs.

Edmunds, George F., Jr.; Jensen, Steven L.; and Berner, Lewis. 1976. *The Mayflies of North and Central America.* Minneapolis: University of Minnesota Press. A scientific reference on American mayflies. Outstanding drawings and notes on natural history of these insects.

Flick, Art, ed. 1972. *Art Flick's Master Fly Tying Guide.* New York: Crown Publishers. A book on fly tying techniques with chapters by many of the best tiers in the United States.

Fulsher, Keith. 1973. *Tying and Fishing the Thunder Creek Series.* Rockville Centre, NY: Freshet Press. Presents some new and significant concepts on imitating forage fishes.

Goddard, John. 1977. *The Super Flies of Still Water.* London: Ernest Benn Limited. Describes the origin, dressing, and manner of presentation for sixty flies that the author considers to be the best for lake fishing.

Gordon, Sid. (1955) 1978 edition. *How to Fish from Top to Bottom.* Stackpole Books, Harrisburg, PA. A text that should be read by every serious fly fisher. This fine book will hone your ability to read the water and find trout.

Harris, J. R. 1956. *An Angler's Entomology.* 2nd ed. New York: A. S. Barnes and Co. A good discussion on the entomology of aquatic insects of the British Isles.

Hilsenhoff, William L. 1977. *Use of Arthropods to Evaluate Water Quality of Streams.* Tech. Bull. 100, Wisconsin Dept. Nat. Res., Madison. Lists many arthropods and their relative tolerances to pollution.

Hubbs, C. L. and Lagler, K. F. 1958. *Fishes of the Great Lakes Region.* Ann Arbor: University of Michigan Press. A good regional guide to freshwater fishes with biological notes.

Jorgenson, Poul. 1973. *Dressing Flies for Fresh and Salt Water.* Rockville Centre, NY: Freshet Press. A good discussion on fly tying by one of the acknowledged masters.

Koch, Ed. 1972. *Fishing the Midge.* Rockville Centre, NY: Freshet Press. A book devoted entirely to imitating and fishing the tiny aquatic insects and crustaceans. A must for anyone interested in this aspect of fly fishing.

La Fontaine, Gary. 1976. *Challenges of the Trout.* Missoula, MT: Mountain Press Publishing Company. Basic information on fly fishing for trout with some good biological insights into the behavior of trout and some of their food organisms.

Leisenring, James and Hidy, Vernon. 1971. *The Art of Tying the Wet Fly and Fishing the Flymph.* New York: Crown Publishers. A true classic by the father of wet fly fishing in America. A book that will never grow old.

Leiser, Eric. 1973. *Fly-Tying Materials.* New York: Crown Publishers. A most useful book on obtaining, preserving, and caring for fly tying materials.

McClane, Al. (1953) 1975 edition. *The Practical Fly Fisherman.* Englewood Cliffs, NJ: Prentice-Hall, Inc. A book that was beyond its time. A classic that should be read and reread by anglers.

Marinaro, Vincent. (1950) 1970 edition. *A Modern Dry Fly Code.* New York: Crown Publishers. The book that established terrestrials as an important part of fly fishing.

————. 1976. *In the Ring of the Rise.* New York: Crown Publishers. A pictorial essay on the feeding of trout with good insights into fly fishing.

Merritt, R. W. and Cummins, K.W. 1978. *An Introduction to the Aquatic Insects of North America.* Dubuque, IA: Kendall/Hunt Publishing Company. The single best identification key to aquatic insects. Keys are to family level (a few to genus). Contains over one thousand superb line drawings and a great deal of natural history.

Ovington, Ray. (1952) 1974 edition. *How to Take Trout on Wet Flies and Nymphs.* Rockville Centre, NY: Freshet Press. A fine discussion of tactics and insect biology.

Pennak, Robert W. 1953. *Fresh Water Invertebrates of the United States.* New York: Ronald Press Company. For years this was the standard text. Some of the classification is now outdated, but this book still contains more on the biology of freshwater invertebrates than any other single source.

Rosborough, E. H. "Polly." (1965) 1978 edition. *Tying and Fishing the Fuzzy Nymphs.* Harrisburg, PA: Stackpole Books. One of the classic texts on fly fishing. By all means read it. Lots of information on tying and fishing nymphs.

Ross, Herbert H. (1944) 1972 edition. *The Caddis Flies or Trichoptera of Illinois.* Entomological Reprint Specialists, Los Angeles. Some of the classification is out of date, but this is still the best book for identification of caddis adults to the genus and species level.

Sawyer, Frank. (1958) 1970 edition. *Nymphs and the Trout.* New York: Crown Publishers. Sawyer is recognized as one of the pioneers of nymph fishing. This volume has a bit on history, a bit on tackle, and solid instruction on tying and fishing Sawyer's patterns.

Schwiebert, Ernest. 1955. *Matching the Hatch.* New York: MacMillan Company. The book that ushered in the modern era of fly fishing in the United States. This text will stand forever as a timeless classic.

———. 1973. *Nymphs.* New York: Winchester Press. An excellent text on the sub-aquatic forms found in trout streams of the United States. Also contains a treasure of nymphing information by one of the greatest anglers of our time.

———. 1978. *Trout.* New York: E. P. Dutton and Company, Inc. A book without equal for sheer volume of comprehensive information on fly fishing for trout. Covers *all* aspects of fly fishing as only Schwiebert can.

Skues, G. E. M. 1949. *The Way of a Trout with a Fly.* 4th ed. London: A. and C. Black. A text that can never age because it contains so many basic insights into trout fishing. Skues is acknowledged as one of the great masters, and this book supports that opinion.

Solomon, Larry and Leiser, Eric. 1977. *The Caddis and the Angler.* Harrisburg, PA: Stackpole Books. An important book because it is the first angling text aimed exclusively at the caddisflies. Good discussions of life cycles, tackle, tying techniques, and angling tactics.

Swan, Lester A. and Papp, Charles S. 1972. *The Common Insects of North America.* New York: Harper and Row, Publishers. Good basic biology and natural history of many insects.

Swisher, Doug and Richards, Carl. 1971. *Selective Trout.* New York: Crown Publishers. The book that established the no-hackle concept in modern fly tying. Also an authoritative study on mayfly hatches of the United States.

———. 1975. *Fly Fishing Strategy.* New York: Crown Publishers. Discusses the concepts of stillborn flies and dry nymphs. Also a good discussion on casting.

Troth, Al. 1978. "Daddy Long Legs." *Fly Tyer* 1, 3:24–25. Describes the tying and fishing techniques for the Troth Super Skater.

Van Put, Ed. 1979. "High-Water Trout." *Rod and Reel* 1, 2:26–31. An interesting article on nymph fishing during high water conditions.

Walker, E. M. 1953. *The Odonata of Canada and Alaska. Part I, General; Part II, The Zygoptera — damselflies.* Vol. I. University of Toronto Press. Good keys and good discussions on these insects.

Waters, Thomas F. 1972. "The Drift of Stream Insects." *Annual Review of Entomology* 17: 253–272. The latest, most complete review of the drift phenomenon.

West, Howard. 1978. "Genetic Hackle." in *The Second Fly-Tyer's Almanac,* ed. by Robert H. Boyle and Dave Whitlock. Philadelphia: J. B. Lippincott Company. This chapter is a superb discussion on the why and wherefore of selecting good quality hackle. Contains some very informative history on modern hackle raisers.

Wetzel, Charles. 1955. *Trout Flies: Naturals and Imitations.* Harrisburg, PA: Stackpole Books. An angling text by an entomologist. Sound information.

Wiggins, Glen B. 1977. *Larvae of North American Caddisfly Genera (Trichoptera).* University of Toronto Press. The most up-to-date information on taxonomy and biology of this important group of insects.

Wright, Leonard. 1972. *Fishing the Dry Fly as a Living Insect.* New York: E. P. Dutton and Co. A thought-provoking book that shatters the myth of the dead drift.

REFERENCES AND KEYS FOR IDENTIFICATION
OF THE FOOD ORGANISMS OF THE TROUT

Borror, D. J. and De Long, D. M. 1964. *An Introduction to the Study of Insects.* Revised ed. New York: Holt, Rinehart and Winston. Contains a good discussion of the biology of the various orders of insects, good keys, and fine drawings.

Burks, B. D. (1953) 1975 edition. *The Mayflies or Ephemeroptera of Illinois.* Los Angeles: Entomological Reprint Specialists. A classic in entomological literature. Some taxonomy is outdated, but the basic materials on structure and biology are sound.

Burt, William H. 1957. See general bibliography.

Caucci, Al and Nastasi, Bob. 1975. See general bibliography.

Chu, H. F. 1949. *How to Know the Immature Insects.* Dubuque, IA: William C. Brown Company. Strictly a key, but has good drawings.

Comstock, J. H. 1948. *An Introduction to Entomology.* 9th ed. Ithaca, NY: Comstock Publishing Company. An indepth introduction to insects.

Eddy, Samuel. 1969. *How to Know the Freshwater Fishes.* Dubuque, IA: William C. Brown Company. A key with very good line drawings.

Edmunds, George F., Jr. et al. 1976. See general bibliography.

Frison, T. H. 1942. "Studies of North American Plecoptera with Special Reference to the Fauna of Illinois." *Bull. Ill. Nat. Hist. Survey* 22: article 2. A fine treatise on the stoneflies. Superb drawings and good biological data are very useful.

Hichcock, Stephen W. 1974. *Guide to the Insects of Connecticut. Part VII: The Plecoptera or Stoneflies of Connecticut.* Bulletin 107, State Geo. and Nat. Hist. Survey of Conn. An excellent, up-to-date key to stoneflies and their biology.

Hilsenhoff, William L. 1975. *Aquatic Insects of Wisconsin.* Technical Bulletin 89, Wisconsin Department of Natural Resources, Madison. Completely illustrated key to genera of aquatic nymphs and larvae. Also contains some very useful biological notes. Taxonomy is current.

Hubbs, C. L. and Lagler, K. F. 1958. See annotated bibliography.

Jacques, H. E. 1947. *How to Know the Insects.* Dubuque, IA: William C. Brown Company. A good key to major insect groups. Good drawings.

———. 1951. *How to Know the Beetles.* Dubuque, IA: William C. Brown Company. Has good drawings of the various aquatic beetle larvae.

Leonard, Justin W. and Leonard, Fannie A. 1962. *Mayflies of Michigan Trout Streams.* Bloomfield Hills, MI: Cranbrook Institute of Science. This classic work has served as a foundation for many anglers. Fine drawings and photographs complement the text. There are good biological notes. Some taxonomy is outdated (at the family level).

McClane, A. J., ed. 1974. *McClane's New Standard Fishing Encyclopedia and International Angling Guide.* New York: Holt, Rinehart, and Winston. A massive, thorough volume that contains excellent information on all phases of fly fishing from how to do it to where to go. Good keys to mayflies and stoneflies. A wealth of biological information on fishes and insects.

Merritt, R. W. and Cummins, K. W., ed. 1978. See annotated bibliography.

Needham, J. G.; Traver, J. R.; and Hsu, Yin-Chi. (1935) 1972 edition. *The Biology of Mayflies.* Hampton, Eng.: E. W. Classey. The authority on mayflies until the publication of the book by Edmunds et al. This book contains a true wealth of information. Some taxonomy is not current.

Pennak, Robert W. 1953. See general bibliography.

Ross, Herbert H. (1944) 1972 edition. See general bibliography.

Swan, L. A. and Papp, C. S. 1972. See general bibliography.

Usinger, R. L., ed. 1963. *Aquatic Insects of California.* Berkeley: University of California Press. Although aimed at California insects, the keys to genera are good for the entire United States. Excellent discussions of the biology of aquatic insects.

Walker, E. M. 1953. See general bibliography.

Walker, E. M. 1958. *The Odonata of Canada and Alaska. Anisoptera.* vol. 2. University of Toronto Press. A fine treatise on the dragonflies.

Wiggins, Glen B. 1977. See general bibliography.

Index

GARY A. BORGER is an associate professor of botany at the University of Wisconsin Center at Wausau, Wisconsin, and is director of the midwest division of Fenwick Fly Fishing Schools. He is the author of *Nymphing: A Basic Book* and has published articles in *Field and Stream, Fly Fisherman, Rod and Reel, Fly Fisher, Fly Fishing the West, Roundtable,* Fenwick's *Lunker Gazette,* and the *Scientific Anglers Fly Fishing Handbook.* Gary's work is accompanied by the fine line art of Robert H. Pils, his friend and fishing companion who is a professional graphic artist.